In **Women Who Compete,** world-renowned athletes from various fields provide valuable lessons in scaling physical, emotional, and mental barriers to success. They honestly share moments of defeat and victory, showing how mistakes and even failure are a part of the pursuit of excellence. Nancy Thies Marshall also recalls her own experiences as an Olympic gymnast to emphasize the importance of overcoming such obstacles as loneliness, perfectionism, envy, and jealousy. You will discover how belief in yourself and in God are the essentials for turning negatives into positives. The Olympic competitors of the past and present featured here include:

- **Debbie Meyer:** conquering the victim mentality

- **Tai Babilonia:** facing overwhelming disappointment with courage

- **Mary Ayotte:** finding self-assurance through faith

- **Bonnie Blair:** accepting criticism as essential for improvement

- **Jackie Joyner-Kersee:** rising above poverty and tragic circumstances

WOMEN

WHO

COMPETE

WOMEN
WHO
COMPETE

NANCY THIES MARSHALL
AND PAM VREDEVELT

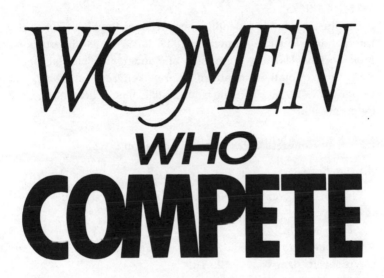

***Power
Books***

FLEMING H. REVELL COMPANY
OLD TAPPAN, NEW JERSEY

Scripture quotations identified NAS are from the New American Standard Bible, © The Lockman Foundation 1960, 1962, 1963, 1968, 1971, 1973, 1975, 1977.

Scripture quotations identified NIV are from the Holy Bible, New International Version. Copyright © 1973, 1978, 1984 International Bible Society. Used by permission of Zondervan Bible Publishers.

Scripture quotations identified TLB are taken from *The Living Bible.* Copyright © 1971 by Tyndale House Publishers, Wheaton, Ill. Used by permission.

Library of Congress Cataloging-in-Publication Data

Marshall, Nancy.
  Women who compete / Nancy Marshall and Pam Vredevelt.
    p.   cm.
  ISBN 0-8007-5277-5
    1. Women athletes—Biography.   2. Competition (Psychology)
I. Vredevelt. Pam W.   . II. Title
GV697.A1M33 1988
796'.092'2—dc19   87-36018
[B]   CIP

Copyright © 1988 by Nancy Thies Marshall and Pam Vredevelt
Published by the Fleming H. Revell Company
Old Tappan, New Jersey 07675
Printed in the United States of America

From Nancy
With Love and Gratitude

To My Grandmothers
Lucille Rankin Webber and Wilma Pattison Player
...My Two Favorite Authors

To My Family
Dick and Marilyn, David and Jodie, Susie, John and
Anne Thies
...Who Embrace Their Own Pursuits of Excellence
With Humility and Integrity,
and Who Challenge Me to Do the Same

To My Husband, Charlie Marshall
...Whose Respect for
People and Commitment to Jesus Christ
Inspire All Who Know Him

From Pam

This Book Is Affectionately Dedicated
to Nancy Thies Marshall
...for Always Being Available
to Help Me Get Back Up

CONTENTS

SEVEN
CURTAILING THE CRUSHING POWER OF CRITICISM

EIGHT
FILLING THE VOID OF LONELINESS

NOTES

PREFACE

IT HAS BEEN two years since Pam and I sat in the church nursery with our newborn children and I shared my ideas for the contents of this manuscript. Having read Pam's other books, I admired her journalistic talent and hoped she would have time in her busy schedule to review my work. I was extremely honored when she agreed to coauthor this book.

From that first day, Pam's endless enthusiasm, discipline, and insight have carried our partnership. Though most of the book is written in first person, her expertise as a Christian therapist, author, and speaker has added depth, biblical perspective, and credibility to the chapters that follow. She has edited and stylized each page for continuity and flow, and in many cases, authored entire sections. Pam has patiently nurtured and encouraged me through each revision. I am deeply indebted to her for her faithful commitment to me and to this project.

Pam and I are fortunate to have many other "partners" who helped us move beyond a rough draft stage. Bill Petersen and the Fleming H. Revell family believed in us and gave us the open door to "go for it." Dick Sleeper, Liz Haney, Sharon Donahue, Roy Carlisle, Sharon Peters, and Ted and Diane Roberts stood on the sidelines, cheering us on, when it would have been easy for us to quit. Betty Guse sacrificially entered numerous revisions into "MAC," our sometimes not-so-cooperative computer.

John Thies, Dave Hastings, Jack Agen, Duane Brady, Veronica Pearcy, Vicki Barram, Susie Thies, and Dick Thies provided significant input as proofreaders. Anne Thies and Jill Welker helped research the profiles of athletes. David and Jodie Thies offered valuable advice on the direction and content of the book. We are especially indebted to Marilyn Thies, who contributed countless hours of all of the above with the love and sensitivity that comes only from a mother.

We extend our sincere gratitude to all of the sports figures whose stories are included here. We thank them for graciously taking time out of busy schedules to share their thoughts and feelings about significant experiences in their lives. Although some of the profiles were compiled from newspaper and magazine articles, all of the subjects are to be admired for their openness and transparency.

Since both Pam and I are mothers of toddlers, free time is at a premium. We are very appreciative of the following people who lovingly befriended our children and spent hours with them so that we could write: Kelly Northcraft; Joanne Dehart; Jerry, Marjie, Rob, Kathie, and Peggy Anderson; Aunt Marilyn and cousins Kristen and Emily Vancil; Dan, Vicki, Wendy, Jeb, and Jill Barram; Janna Romig; Terry and Teresa Hancock.

Ginny Seipt and Charlie Jones are two former colleagues at NBC Sports, whose genuine respect for the humanness of athletes sparked a desire in me to write about the emotional hurdles facing anyone pursuing excellence. My involvement with the people and ministry of Young Life has shaped my thinking and confirmed the value of many of the principles that follow for overcoming those hurdles.

I also extend heartfelt thanks to Bill and Barbara Marshall, Jeff and Marilyn Vancil, and Greg and Nancy Marshall. I was fortunate to marry into a family so eager to offer encouragement and support.

Other family members who were a source of renewed inspiration for the ongoing task of completing this manuscript include J.J. and Kurtis Vancil, Aaron and Brooke Marshall, Stephanie, Daniel, and Michael Thies, Chuck and Dana Walker, and Dottie and Jim Walker.

In preparing this manuscript, many hours were spent scrounging through letters, diaries, and scrapbooks collected during my competitive years. I have relived my athletic career, event by event, emotion by emotion.

Many of the valuable lessons I learned during that season of my life were taught by people who willingly walked with me during my quest for athletic excellence.

I want to give particular thanks to my coaches Dick and Linda Mulvihill and the staff at the McKinley YMCA in Champaign-Urbana, Illinois, and at the National Academy of Artistic Gymnastics in Eugene, Oregon. Space does not allow me to name the many other coaches and officials who influenced my career. I am grateful for the selfless ways they gave of themselves so that I might pursue my goals.

Since many of the personal accounts in the following pages focus on my participation in the 1972 Olympic Games, I also want to express appreciation to my Olympic teammates: Kim Chase, Debbie Hill, Linda Metheny, Joan Moore, Roxanne Pierce, and Cathy Rigby, whose determination and perseverance gave me an experience worth writing about.

Anyone pursuing excellence knows the value of "balcony people." My support team throughout my competitive years was full of friends standing in the balcony, cheering me on through triumphs and despair. Some of those loyal "team members" include Dan and Marge Perrino, Terry and Nancy Davis, George and Miriam Hunt, Mildred Barnett, and Louise Woodruffe, who filled my scrapbooks with countless letters of affirmation and gifts of love which continue to encourage me today. Debbie Jackson, Jill Welker, Bonnie Green, Jodie Peressini, and Vicki Miller were peers who allowed me to be real and loved me in spite of my big ears and acne. Their friendship convinced me of the need for chapter 8.

Pam and I are abundantly blessed to have so many family members who are our most committed cheerleaders and whose quest for excellence in their own lives has been a daily inspiration to us. With respect and admiration, we recognize our grandparents: Dave and Wilma Player, Charlie and Lucille Webber, Jim and Dottie Walker, and Carl and Olive Dalton; and aunts and uncles who, along with their children, have surrounded our pursuits with love and encouragement: Dave and Beth Player, Jennifer and Jim Zaccagni, Craig and Alice Webber, Carl and Cathie Webber, Jim and Charlene Walker, Jim and Janis Miller, and Barb Walker; and other relatives who have contributed special support: Claire Manning and Karen Beardsley.

My Olympic journey and subsequent endeavors have indeed been a family affair. With sincere humility, I thank Mom and Dad, David, Susie, John, and Anne, who traveled the road with me, believed in me, and who all sacrificed without complaint so that my dreams could become a reality.

I mentioned earlier that this book has been two years in the making. Our helpless newborns are now rambunctious, joyful toddlers. We are most grateful to Ryan and Jessie for confirming that stumbling and falling is part of growing up, and that the only way to overcome obstacles in life is to get back up and try again.

Pam and I owe the largest debt of all to our husbands, Charlie and John, who listened, encouraged, patiently persevered, and with the loving hearts of servants, unquestioningly relieved us of the duties of motherhood so that we could complete the manuscript. Charlie and John share our prayer that all who read this will be challenged to pursue God's best for their lives.

Nancy

Dear Mom, Dad, Chuck, and Kelly,

I am indebted to you for your unselfish love and loyalty to me. Thank you for your unswerving commitment to support God's purposes in my life. I love you.

Pam

WOMEN
WHO
COMPETE

ONE

BREAKING BARRICADES OF DOUBT

THE BUS WAS late and I stood stranded in the Olympic Village with my six U.S. teammates. Our competition in the 1972 Olympic Games was to begin in just over an hour. We waited impatiently for some sign of transportation, realizing our warm-up time slipped away with each passing moment. With no bus in sight, we opted to jog the half mile from the athletes' village to the arena.

"What a great way to start out the most exciting day of my life!" I grunted as we wove our way through sports fans on hand in Munich for the Summer Games. "Not exactly first-class treatment!"

My eyes focused on the two "senior" members of our

team running in front of me. I admired Linda Metheny and Cathy Rigby. In many ways they were my idols.

It seems like yesterday when I watched their performances in the 1968 Olympics on TV, I thought as we left the entrance to the village and picked up speed on the open sidewalks. Participating in the Olympics had seemed like an impossibility for me in 1968. It was a realistic dream for others but not for me, eleven-year-old Nancy Thies. I didn't think I had much natural talent. I was pudgy and not very flexible or physically strong. For a gymnast, those characteristics spelled mediocrity.

But soon after the '68 games my coach, Dick Mulvihill, approached me with a challenge. "Hey Nancy, come over here," he called from the corner of the gym. *What does he want?* I wondered.

Perched on a simple folding chair, he asked me to climb up on his knee for a "heart to heart." As an eleven-year-old, I felt totally embarrassed.

I'm too grown up for this, I thought. *I wish he would hurry and get it over with!* I must have turned ten shades of purple.

Curious, I listened to one of Dick's famous pep talks. He was beginning a four-year training program to prepare the next crop of youngsters for the 1972 Olympics.

With his eye-to-eye approach, he looked at me hard and said, "Nancy, you have the potential to make the U.S. Olympic team in four years. By 1972 you'll be fifteen and old enough to compete. If you really apply yourself in these next four years, you can become an Olympian!"

Though he spoke intensely, I didn't take him seriously. I kept thinking, *He's giving all of my teammates the same spiel. I'm not really that good . . . he's just saying that to be nice.*

Dick's local YMCA program was not any ordinary recreational program. He was considered by many one of the best gymnastics coaches in the country. Three of our team members had just returned from competing in the Olympics in Mexico City. One of them, Linda Metheny, was also the U.S. National Champion. We usually won every meet we entered. I was surrounded by the best.

Dick's years of coaching gave him a discerning eye that saw beyond the rough edges of my abilities. He had an uncanny sense of foresight. In his eyes I was not just an Illinois schoolgirl, but rather Olympic material he wanted to train for Munich.

Soon after Dick's talk, I found myself facing the first major hurdle in my quest to become an Olympian: DOUBT. I couldn't see myself going to the Olympics. Why me? I was the one on the team with two left feet. But I had a choice, a decision to make, as I struggled with doubt during the pre-Olympic years. I could either dwell on my weaknesses and lose sight of my goals, or believe my coach when he said, "Nancy, to achieve

excellence in any pursuit, *you must first believe in yourself.*
You've got what it takes. Believe it, and go for it!"

Dick was no amateur. His track record of coaching
Olympians proved his words were not empty jargon.
Accepting his counsel sparked a new level of confidence
that enabled me to clear the hurdle of self-doubt. Four
years later I arrived at the athletes' entrance to the
Sporthalle in Munich, out of breath but ready to compete in the Olympic Games.

Do you have difficulty seeing your dreams come true?
Are they up close and in color, or at a distance in black
and white? Do you allow others to be mirrors for you,
reflecting your blinded potential? If you identify with
these questions, it is likely your vision is blurred by
doubt.

Perhaps you don't have a mentor like Dick Mulvihill
offering helpful guidance. Qualified experts are hard to
find. Some coaches don't have a discerning eye for raw
talent. If you feel as if you are plodding alone on the
road to success, take heart—there is hope! Record books
are filled with names of once ordinary people who felt
inadequate and doubted their capabilities. Many lacked
support and encouragement from others, yet they
learned to believe in themselves and break the barri-
cades of doubt.

Abraham Lincoln swallowed political defeat seven
times in twenty-eight years before being elected president of the United States in 1860. Though blind and
deaf, Helen Keller committed her life to helping the less

fortunate and became an inspiration to millions. Albert Einstein flunked his college entrance exams, yet developed the complex theory of relativity. Marian Anderson overcame poverty and prejudice to become the first black soloist for the New York City Metropolitan Opera.

How do winners cultivate self-confidence? What enables them to capitalize on their strengths? What motivates them to pursue their dreams? A common thread woven through the lives of many champions is the ability to listen to an inner call to achieve. This calling isn't instilled by a coach, friend, or parent. It is a call that comes from the heart, an insatiable desire to excel that leaves doubt and insecurity at the starting blocks.

A PASSION TO PERFORM

The place is Stockholm, Sweden, 1956. A young Danish equestrian athlete, Lis Hartel, is being draped with her second Olympic silver medal for the dressage event. Lis won her first medal in this exacting discipline, where the horse responds to subtle commands from the rider, in the 1952 Olympics. The flags of the winners' countries are now hoisted, and the national anthem of the gold medalist majestically fills the air. Family members and sporting enthusiasts energetically applaud the achievements of the honored athletes.

It is not unreasonable to assume that many in the crowd view Lis, the recipient of two consecutive silver medals, as a winner blessed with natural talent who encountered few obstacles along her road to victory. But history unveils a different story about Lis and her horse, Gigolo. Let's visit her twelve years prior to this award ceremony.

The year was 1944. As a happy wife, mother of one child and pregnant with another, Lis was high on life. She was young, healthy, strong, and had a promising future as one of the best riders in Denmark.

But one morning she awoke with a sore neck and an excruciating headache. Within a few days paralysis consumed her entire body. Doctors diagnosed polio and offered little encouragement for recovery. "At best, you might be able to walk with two canes, Lis. . . ." In disbelief, her emotions ran wild and unchecked when she heard the prognosis. Fearing the possible death of her unborn child, and facing a seemingly hopeless situation, despair held hostage the athletic dreams Lis had embraced for so many years.

Lying in her hospital bed, Lis could not prevent her imagination from wandering to the familiar riding course that was a second home for her. She pictured herself guiding Gigolo by the gentle, firm touch of her thigh and knee muscles. But her daydreams changed midstream when the cold reality of her circumstances resurfaced. She now had no sensation in those muscles.

No one expected Lis to ride again. It would be a major accomplishment just to learn to function from a wheel-chair. Her limited body control and mobility were definite handicaps for the precision of the dressage event. With her dreams destroyed by a disease, with an uncertain future ahead, Lis could easily have stepped off the road to athletic success. Yet she felt compelled to ride. Eventually the overwhelming doubts paled in light of her burning passion to perform with Gigolo. Resolving that her recovery would not be complete until she rode again, she set her mind to press forward.

Her first priority was to leave the hospital for home, where she could work more intensely on a rehabilitation program. Aside from the physical therapy regimen prescribed by her doctors, Lis's husband and mother rigged up a homemade weight system so sensitive that it could detect the smallest muscle movement of an arm or leg. Lis worked to achieve slight sensations in her limbs. First there was nothing. And then finally her right arm moved! At last, there was hope!

Lis was fervently committed to relearning muscle control, even though progress was painfully slow. After gaining partial movement in her arms and legs, she had to learn to sit up. Then came another challenge: she needed more rigorous exercise. Her husband and mother connected two stationary bicycles together. The pedaling of one initiated the pedals of the other. Though she could withstand only a few minutes of this exercise at a time, Lis soon began to sense control in her thigh muscles. All this occurred while she was still pregnant.

Several months later, Lis gave birth to a healthy baby girl, which briefly slowed her recovery progress. But soon she was back at it again. Hours were spent facedown on top of a towel, while her husband and mother lifted each end of the towel off the floor, giving Lis enough support to move forward. From inches to yards, Lis crept a little farther each day.

When her strength was adequate, Lis began efforts to walk. Success was real, although slow and painful. Eight months after Lis was stricken with polio, she was maneuvering around on two crutches. To most people, this accomplishment would mean victory. Yet Lis knew she wouldn't be satisfied until she rode atop Gigolo again.

After much convincing, Lis's family wheeled her out to the stables and helped her mount her horse. She hoped instinct would prevail while the reflexes in her thighs and knees guided them. But instead, she lost her balance and toppled off. Again and again Lis was remounted on Gigolo, only to fall minutes later. Nothing had challenged her mental and physical fortitude more.

Exhausted and discouraged, Lis once asked her husband to hang up her riding gear for good, but her desire to perform brought her back to the stable. In time, her strength and balance returned, and hopes evolved into reality with each new accomplishment. Within a year she was riding on her own.

In 1946, two years after polio was diagnosed, Lis attended the Scandinavian Riding Championships as a spectator. Seeing her old friends and competitors in action made her even more determined to ride in the 1947 championships. And ride she did, finishing second in the women's dressage. Her progress fueled her determination to participate in the Olympics. She maintained a rigorous training schedule, spending hours in physical therapy and working with Gigolo. Her days were full as she juggled the demands of Olympic preparation with mothering two active youngsters.

To compensate for the loss of feeling below her knees, she experimented with alternative methods of riding and developed her own process of training. Five years and two operations later, Lis Hartel qualified as one of the top twenty-four riders in the world in her event and earned the right to compete in the Olympic Games. When the dressage competition was finished, Lis stood tall while receiving the silver medal. She went on to repeat the same feat at the Olympics four years later.

What enabled Lis to overcome the overwhelming doubt and uncertainty she experienced in her hospital room? How was she able to recommit herself to her goals, knowing the road to success would be a grueling, painful endeavor?

Part of the answer lies in Lis's choice to face her doubts and evision her dreams as a reality. It wasn't only in the certainty of her abilities that her passion for riding grew stronger. When Lis's natural abilities ended, she at first experienced doubt. But doubt struggled against those physical limitations and called out for answers. This drove Lis to problem solving, even when no solution seemed possible. Ultimately Lis's doubts became an opportunity for increased faith in her abilities to perform, and prepared the way for her to ride again.

As Lis not only acknowledged her limitations but also listened to the desires of her heart, her passion for riding became a motivating force on days when progress seemed slow and goals unreachable. Her inner call to perform overcame not only the paralyzing effect of self-doubt but also the debilitating blows of her actual paralysis.[1]

FROM HIGH SCHOOL RUNNER-UP TO COLLEGIATE NATIONAL CHAMPION

In more recent years, a determined college gymnast struggled with similar doubts. Mary Ayotte sat in the bleachers of Penn State's Rec Hall during the finals of the 1979 Collegiate National Gymnastics Championships. She had represented Oregon State University in the preliminary rounds of competition but had not done well enough to qualify for the finals.

I'd just die to be out on the floor competing as one of the finalists! she thought. *I wonder if I'll ever be one of the top eight.*

Mary had done reasonably well as a high school gymnast, placing third as a junior and fifth as a senior in the all-around competition of the Oregon State High School Championships. But in spite of earlier accomplishments, she wondered if her dreams of being a top collegiate gymnast would ever become a reality. Mary's abilities varied: she had exceptional strength but she was not very flexible and had little dance background. What confidence she had in her power, she lost the minute she stepped into a dance class. It took her twice as long to learn routines, and she often left the dance floor flooded by waves of insecurity and self-doubt.

While reminiscing about her training, she said, "I hated the days when the choreographer came to work on our new routines for the year. I was always the last one to catch on and felt so uncoordinated!"

Mary wasn't thwarted only by inner feelings of inadequacy. She was also bombarded by negative outside voices. The coaches at the University of Washington and the University of Oregon, her two top collegiate choices, said she probably would not make their teams. "You can try out for the team as a walk-on, but don't get your hopes up. And don't expect any financial help. You're just not good enough to qualify for a scholarship."

Beaten down by disaffirming voices, Mary often thought, *Maybe I'm not as good as I think I am.* . . . But her fighting spirit compelled her to keep looking for a college where she could compete.

That search led her on a recruiting trip to Boise State University, where coach Ed Zimmer spoke the first words of encouragement and affirmation that Mary had heard: "You have such great potential, Mary. You haven't even begun to reach your peak as a gymnast."

Months later she met, in Corvallis, with then Oregon State University coach Ron Ludwig. He demonstrated his own confidence in her abilities by offering Mary a partial scholarship. Since OSU met her academic needs, she signed up to join the Beavers.

Mary's first year was a challenge. She saw each meet as a chance to prove her worth and pressured herself constantly to improve. When the season ended with the final meet, she watched the best collegiate gymnasts in the country battle for top spots at the NCAA meet, wondering if she would ever join their ranks.

She compared her inadequacies to the polished and confident routines of the finalists. *Were those other coaches right? Do I have any natural talent? Will I ever be able to dance with confidence and reach the caliber of these top gymnasts?*

When the finals concluded, Mary headed back to Corvallis, determined to improve her national ranking. In the months that followed, she began to see that her love for performing and her natural edge in the power events were real strengths. Something else also happened in Mary's life that created a unique confidence deep inside her. Through a friend, Mary came to understand that she was created to have a personal relationship with God. As she developed a relationship with Him through Bible study and prayer, confidence became a natural by-product. Self-doubt was gradually replaced by self-assurance. As God's Spirit became more prominent in Mary's life she found that "in reverencing the Lord there is confidence" (*see* Proverbs 14:26 NAS).

Mary's new spiritual confidence affected her overall outlook on life as well as her gymnastic performances. Eventually her self-doubt gave way to dreams of becoming one of the best. During the following competitive seasons Mary inched her way up in the national standings. By her senior year Mary was the star of the Oregon State team and was awarded a complete athletic scholarship. In 1982 she finished third all-around at the Collegiate Nationals and became the National Champion in the floor exercise event. She was also honored with the coveted American Award, which recognizes the outstanding senior collegiate gymnast in the country.

Reflecting on the past, Mary said, "When I look back on my collegiate career, I'm sometimes overwhelmed. By the end of my senior year, I had accomplished much more than I ever thought possible." Mary found that listening to the words of her Creator had sown seeds of faith and confidence within her character.

GOD KNOWS YOUR CAPABILITIES

Do you ever wonder if you are capable of excellence? Are there times when it is difficult to believe in yourself or your abilities? Be encouraged by the fact that God believes in you and wants to place His compassionate hands on your life. He is keenly aware of your needs and wants:

O Lord, you have examined my heart and know everything about me. You know when I sit or stand. When far away you know my every thought. You chart the path ahead of me, and tell me where to stop and rest. Every moment, you know where I am. You know what I am going to say before I even say it. You both precede and follow me, and place your hand of blessing on my head. . . .

You made all the delicate, inner parts of my body, and knit them together in my mother's womb. Thank you for making me so wonderfully complex! It is amazing to think about. Your workmanship is marvelous—how well I know it. You were there while I was being formed in utter seclusion! You saw me before I was born and scheduled each day of my life before I began to breathe. Every day was recorded in your Book!

How precious it is, Lord, to realize that you are thinking about me constantly! I can't even count how many times a day your thoughts turn towards me. And when I waken in the morning, you are still thinking of me!

Psalms 139:1–18 TLB

From the moment of our conception, God was involved in creating each one of us as a masterpiece. God fashioned us in a special way because He wanted us to make a unique statement and to leave an impression on the world we touch. There is no one, and will never be anyone, who is our exact equal. None of us is a mediocre mass market copy, hot off the assembly line. God designed each of us as a divine original, and He longs to have a personal relationship with us. We are constantly on His mind.

When we open ourselves to a relationship with our Creator and cultivate a friendship with Him, the Spirit of God supernaturally instills confidence in our spirit. He energizes us with power and strength beyond our own abilities, a power that can help uncoordinated dancers to become National Floor Exercise Champions.

Mary Ayotte testified to this: "My relationship with the Lord enabled me to be a much better gymnast than I ever would have been depending on my own abilities alone."

Regardless of the particular path we walk in life, we all face moments when self-doubt threatens to destroy our dreams. What mother hasn't doubted her abilities to raise rambunctious two-year-olds into well-adjusted adults? What businessman hasn't felt his stomach turn when a transaction hangs in the balance? What teenager hasn't questioned his acceptance among his peers?

It is during stressful times, when turbulent emotions make it difficult for us to believe in ourselves, that we need to *listen to the experts:* their advice and encouragement is backed by years of proven experience; *listen to the desires of our hearts:* the human will can diminish the height of hurdles we face; and *listen to our Creator and build a friendship with Him:* self-doubt melts away as His presence builds confidence and security within our spirit.

TWO

SOFTENING THE BLOWS OF INJUSTICE

INJUSTICE IS ONE of the most common hurdles we face in life and is no respecter of persons. This unexpected and undeserved obstacle often takes dreams and reduces them to thoughts of what might have been. It can contradict what is right and predictable and temporarily halt anyone in the pursuit of excellence.

My first unforgettable brush with injustice came early in my athletic career. Southern Illinois University hosted the qualification trials for the Pan American Games team in 1971. During this particular year, the athletes were told that the top seven competitors would represent the United States at the Pan Am Games. Those placing eighth through fourteenth would compete as a team in Europe that same summer.

I didn't have any illusions of making the Pan Am team. At thirteen, I was still quite young and inexperienced compared with other competitors. But I did think I had a chance to win a place on the European tour team.

The qualification trial was my first major senior national meet. Until that time, I had trained in the shadow of top gymnasts. This was my big opportunity to compete with them on the same level. Filled with nervous optimism, I headed off to Carbondale with my teammates.

When the chalk dust had settled and the scores were tallied, all five gymnasts from my team, the McKinley YMCA, had placed among the top fourteen spots. This account appeared in our local newspaper:

> Tuscola's Linda Metheny and Champaign's Theresa Fileccia earned berths on the 1971 United States women's gymnastics team, which will compete in the Pan American Games in Colombia this summer.
>
> Three other members of the McKinley YMCA women's gymnastic team earned berths on the United States national team with their performances in the team trials staged at Southern Illinois University. Kathy Stewart, Jody Peressini, and Nancy Thies joined Linda and Theresa on the national team.[1]

I had finally done it! I had made a United States national team! On top of that, I was going to get to compete internationally. For the first time in my gymnastics career, I felt I had tasted success. Finishing thirteenth in the nation bolstered my confidence. With a new bounce in my step, I returned home to prepare energetically for competing in Europe.

I was quickly caught up in all the excitement of preparing for international competition. First I secured a passport, since I had never before been out of the country. Next, my mom and I went shopping to collect all of the necessities for a trip abroad. Thanks to the local publicity about the upcoming competition, I enjoyed being somewhat of a celebrity among my peers at the junior high school. Friends and family alike were beaming proudly about my accomplishments and enthusiastically sharing my excitement about competing in Europe.

The weeks passed swiftly as we continued to train each day. Although workouts were long and hard, visions of Europe lessened the fatigue from practices.

Life was like a fairy tale. It seemed I had everything going for me. At thirteen, I was thirteenth in the nation among gymnasts. My friends at school thought I was famous. My family had committed themselves to make all the sacrifices necessary for me to excel. What else could a young girl want?

But then one of those humbling episodes in life snatched me out of the clouds of stardom and jolted me back to reality. About three weeks before I was to leave the country, Mom and Dad received a phone call from my assistant coach.

In an apprehensive and apologetic voice she said, "I just received word from the United States Gymnastics Federation Office that Nancy will not be representing the U.S. in the European competition this summer. Instead, they have decided to take another girl in her place. The coach traveling with the team requested that one of the girls from her own club compete as a member of the team." (This girl had placed twenty-third in the qualification trials, while I had placed thirteenth!)

I'll never forget the afternoon my parents broke the news to me. My first reaction was to think, *This can't happen to me! It's not fair. I'm certain they have made a mistake. They'll see how wrong they are and place me back on the team!*

Those hopes never materialized. I left the kitchen that afternoon with my mind in a blur. It seemed that all my dreams of world travel and international competition had been dashed against a rock, with pieces scattered in every direction.

Over and over again I kept saying, "It's not fair . . . it's not fair!"

I must have cried for a week. I wasn't prepared for the humiliation accompanying this injustice. All the news articles, the fanfare, the hard training, seemed meaningless. One minute everything was great. One phone call later, my world had crumbled.

I tried to find a way to justify my loss, but there wasn't a logical or fair explanation. I felt cheated. It seemed as if this decision had been arbitrarily made, with little thought or consideration. In the past, our system for choosing a team in America had always been based on qualification trials. This was one safeguard that ensured some degree of objectivity in the selection process. I had earned the right to compete in Europe at the trials. Why the switch?

All I could think at the time was, *This is a royal rip-off!*

I doubt that the officials who made the determination ever knew how deeply it affected me. I still wonder if they ever really considered the consequences of their ruling before calling my coach. Little did they know their decision taught me one of the most important lessons I've ever learned. It was at this time in my life that I came face-to-face with a hard reality: *Life is not always fair.*

I don't think there is a person reading this who hasn't known, firsthand, the bitter taste of injustice. To one degree or another, we have all experienced the painfully familiar sting of unfair circumstances.

It is easy to miss the lessons that can be learned from situations like these because we have a hard time believing anything of value can be gleaned from something unfair. Good and injustice seem to be opposites. But because we live in an imperfect world, we can't escape the pain of unfair circumstances on our journey through life. The innocent will sometimes be victims of deep heartache. Not everything in life is fair or predict-able. Many wrongs are not made right. There will be times when each of us has questions and no answers.

An important question is, can tough circumstances be beneficial? Is it possible for an injustice to work to our advantage? Events in the lives of others teach us that something good can come from inequitable situations as we search for the positive hidden in the negative.

THE INJUSTICE OF INJURY

"Sue, your ankles are not healing. The impact from the hard landings in gymnastics is too extreme. You must choose between gymnastics or the ability to walk later in life."

As Sue Soffe's doctor spoke, angry questions darted back and forth in her mind with no logical progression. *Why should I have to give up the sport I love? Why does one injury have to ruin my entire career? Why did this freak accident have to happen to me?*

A few weeks earlier, Sue had landed wrong in a vaulting routine and broken both ankles. Though she worked daily to rehabilitate her ankles, progress was virtually nonexistent.

Gymnastics had been Sue's life. As a youngster she showed great promise. Her natural flexibility and slen-der body made the sport easy for her. She was known for approaching each event with dogged determination and never giving less than 100 percent. But after years of sacrifice, a slight miscalculation on a landing brought her athletic development to a screeching halt. Now she had to make a choice. Hobbling out of the medical clinic, she thought she was doomed to an unwanted divorce from the sport she deeply loved.

A ray of hope pierced her gloom when Alla Svirsky, a Russian-born athlete-turned-coach, appeared at practice one afternoon. She asked Sue to consider a career in rhythmic gymnastics. This distant cousin of artistic gymnastics is performed on the floor exercise mat and doesn't punish the athlete's body to the degree that the artistic form does. Using a hoop, rope, ball, ribbon, or clubs, the gymnast creatively dances and does basic tumbling moves to musical accompaniment.

Initially Sue wasn't interested. She had seen a demonstration of rhythmic gymnastics before, and it wasn't appealing to her, but she didn't want to give up the sport completely. Rhythmic gymnastics was one way to remain in active competition. Overcoming her doubts, she decided to give it a try.

After some time off for recuperation, Sue started workouts once again. During the first few practices, she had a hard time bypassing the bars and balance beam.

"I couldn't stay off the stuff. Whenever I was in the gym it was like the equipment stood there calling my name. I hated being yanked off it," she said, "even though I knew it was for my own good."[2]

Eventually Sue transferred her complete attention from artistic gymnastics to mastering new routines as a rhythmic gymnast. Her efforts were rewarded when, in her first California State meet, she finished eighth. In the following regional competition, she jumped to third place. Six years later, her doubtful beginnings triumphantly culminated in six National Championships and a gold medal at the 1978 Pan Pacific International Championships. Sue was the first American to take home the gold in an international competition for rhythmic gymnastics.

Life taught Sue an important truth: The possibility of new experiences and rewards often follows closely after an injustice. These new experiences can contribute color to our character and enrich our journey through life. When Sue risked walking through the door Alla Svirsky held open for her, she found a whole new world, and the injustice lost its impact.

BURNED BY THE BOYCOTT

Injustice is a familiar word to the athletes on the 1980 U.S. Summer Olympic Team. Lifelong dreams of competing in the Olympic Games turned into a nightmare when, in response to the Soviets' refusal to move their troops out of Afghanistan, President Jimmy Carter called for a boycott of the Moscow Games. Whether or not U.S. team members agreed with the principles behind their nonparticipation, all were stripped of the rare chance of Olympic competition, with no voice in the matter.

The devastating impact of this decision was succinctly communicated by Women's Volleyball Coach Arie Selinger: "It was the equivalent of going through school and the last day the dean calls you in and says you won't be getting your diploma."[3]

Selinger and his team of fifteen women had every reason to be disappointed. They had given up families, schooling, and jobs to train together year-round at the Olympic training center in Colorado Springs. Their undying commitment had brought them from a team that didn't qualify for the '76 Games to one of the top-ranked women's volleyball teams in the world. Sports enthusiasts recognized the team as a legitimate contender for a medal in Moscow.

The Saturday the boycott was official, these athletes stood together in the gym empty-handed, having exchanged four to eight years of their lives for unfulfilled goals. Veteran Debbie Landreth was furious.

> I had done everything possible to reach my goal. I was in peak condition, prepared for every possible scenario. I thought I had my bases covered. I knew I could overcome sickness, injury, or fatigue . . . but I never dreamed the team would be stopped by a boycott. There was *nothing* anyone could do to change the circumstances.
>
> More than anything, I wanted a tangible reason why it happened. I guess I expected God to explain it to me or to replace my loss with something better.

I may never fully understand the situation, but I do know that I have grown and changed. I'm convinced I'm a better coach and more conscientious about preparing my athletes for hardship. I try to emphasize that no one can promise fairness because there will always be circumstances over which we have no control.

When an injustice affects her athletes, Debbie is able to soften the blow. "I can empathize with them. I know the emotions they are feeling, and they know I've walked the same path of frustration. My words don't change the circumstances, but at least I can offer hope for brighter tomorrows."

Debbie's life has indeed been filled with bright tomorrows. In 1981 she married sportswriter Dennis Brown, and in 1983 she became the head women's volleyball coach at Arizona State University. Debbie's coaching expertise was confirmed in 1987 when she was voted the Pac 10 Conference Volleyball Coach of the Year and named to the coaching staff for the 1988 U.S. Olympic Team.

There is no way of knowing who the medalists would have been in the 1980 Olympics. No doubt the U.S. Women's Volleyball Team would have bettered any previous finish. Unfortunately, the boycott snatched the satisfaction of that accomplishment from a team of dedicated athletes. But, as one of those athletes struggled to understand the heartache of her circumstances, she gained more than an Olympic medal. Debbie Lan-

dreth developed a lifelong sensitivity to the disappointment of injustice that added depth to her character and
skill to her coaching abilities.

Today she instills in other young women a will to
persevere, the patience to endure, and the hope for
good things to come. Those qualities don't always
guarantee gold medals, but they go a lot further in
equipping young athletes for the realities of a not-so-
perfect world.

LETDOWN AT LAKE PLACID

Tai Babilonia, a striking young nineteen-year-old figure skater, stood alongside her partner, Randy Gardner,
facing 450 journalists in the Lake Placid, New York,
high school gymnasium. This chilly Saturday morning
was only the midpoint of the 1980 Winter Olympic
Games, but for Tai and Randy, the search for Olympic
gold was over. Fielding questions from reporters, they
tried to communicate the emotion-packed events of the
past few days. To appreciate this moment in history,
let's look at the journey that brought them to this final
destination of their amateur careers.

The road to the 1980 Olympics had been unusually
long for Tai. She first started skating competitively in
1969 at the tender age of eight. Four years later her coach,
John Nicks, advised her to leave singles skating for couples competition. Teaming up with Randy Gardner, she
trained six days a week from 5:45 A.M. to 2:00 P.M.

The switch paid off. In 1973, Tai and Randy won the U.S. Junior National Pairs title. A year later, they placed second at the Senior National Championships and qualified to represent the United States at the 1974 World Figure Skating Championships.

At the competition, Dick Button, a two-time Olympic skating gold medalist and television analyst, said, "Tai and Randy are at least two or three years ahead of their time. It's hard to take your eyes off Tai."[4]

Button's words emphasized the wealth of talent each performer possessed, and skating aficionados predicted that Tai and Randy would end the Soviet domination of world pairs skating. The dynamic couple's accomplishments in the following years only whetted their appetites for Olympic gold.

In the 1976 Olympics, Tai and Randy finished fifth. After the Games, they captured four U.S. Pairs titles, and in 1979 won the World Figure Skating Championships in Vienna, Austria. This ended the fourteen-year reign of Soviet World Pair champions. It had been twenty-nine years since U.S. athletes grabbed the top spot in international competition. As the Olympics approached, the stage was set for the classic confrontation between the reigning World Champions, Tai and Randy, and the former World Champions from the Soviet Union, Irina Rodnina and Aleksandr Zaitsev.

Not only did Tai and Randy face the challenge of defending their world title in the '80 Olympics but this was also their last and best chance for an Olympic medal, the ultimate achievement for any world-class athlete. Eleven years of training and sacrifice had prepared them for this final competition, and they had high hopes for the gold.

Shortly before leaving their homes in Los Angeles, California, for Lake Placid, Randy pulled a groin muscle during practice. Within a few days his pain subsided, but both skaters knew the injury would make their Olympic quest more difficult. With cautious enthusiasm they left for the Olympic Games.

From the moment they arrived at the Olympic Village, it was virtually impossible to escape probing reporters eager for fresh tidbits of information. Publicly Tai and Randy minimized Randy's injury. But privately they both dreaded the possibility of a forced withdrawal from competition.

Two days before the pairs competition, Randy pulled the muscle again. He tried to shrug off the injury, insisting to the press he would be okay. Doctors gave him painkillers to ease the discomfort, but both gold-medal hopefuls knew their chances of performing were slim.

Warming up on the ice at the Olympic field house that Friday night, Randy fell three times and came close to dropping Tai once. More than nine thousand people in the arena and millions watching on television waited on the edge of their seats to see if the reigning World Champions would compete.

After the third pair of skaters finished their performance, Tai and Randy skated on to the ice once more for a short warm-up; when Randy fell after a simple jump, Coach Nicks beckoned them to the sidelines and voiced the inevitable: "It's too dangerous for you to skate, Randy."

In the arena where they thought their dreams would become reality, Tai and Randy made one of the most painful decisions of their lives. They withdrew from the competition.

Undoubtedly both skaters had many questions with no answers. Those following the careers of these two young athletes, watching history unfold that Friday night, also wrestled with disappointment: How could this happen? Certainly injury is a part of athletics, but why now? They had dedicated their lives to this dream . . . it just wasn't fair! How could Tai and Randy leave Lake Placid feeling good about their skating careers?

While Randy struggled with the consequences of his injury, Tai experienced a unique sense of grief. She was healthy, in top condition, and primed for the best performance of her life. Yet the door for earning a gold medal was slammed in her face.

Tai recalls, "It was hard to feel anything during the hours that followed. I felt like I was in the middle of a nightmare . . . I kept wishing I'd wake up and none of it would have happened."

Despite their disappointment, the two skaters graciously talked with journalists from around the world on Saturday morning. Tai had been up most of the night with her twenty-three-year-old brother, Constancio, trying to make sense of the whole ordeal. In the early-morning hours, thanks to his encouragement and the hundreds of telegrams from friends and fans, Tai made her first efforts to crawl out of her depression: "I started telling myself that I had so much ahead of me and not to let one disappointment ruin the rest of my life."

No, they didn't win any medals at the last amateur competition. No, they did not even compete. But both skaters could recall many treasured memories from the time they spent together over the years.

"We've traveled to Russia and Japan. We've met the Queen of England, and much, much more." They assured reporters, "It has been worth it all!"

Instead of dwelling on what they didn't achieve, Tai and Randy chose to be grateful for their experiences and what they had attained. That choice didn't change their circumstances, but it did soften the blow of their injustice and tame the anger that could have run wild. And it enabled them to walk through the next few weeks and months with grace and courage.

As with most life-altering experiences, time tempers the pain of unfulfilled goals. Today, Tai speaks joyfully about what has transpired in the years since Lake Placid:

> Randy and I have a depth and a quality to our
> friendship that is only there because we've worked

through our disappointment together. I've seen Randy struggle with guilt and regret, and I have so much respect for him. He has dealt honestly and courageously with pressures from the public and press. He could easily have given up, but he didn't. His determination to train after the whole ordeal is to be admired. I deeply appreciate his commitment to our careers as pair skaters.

The injustice Tai Babilonia and Randy Gardner suffered is one that Olympic spectators will not soon forget. Indeed they may be, as one reporter stated, "the most famous Olympic skaters never to have won a medal at the Games."[5] Today, as professional skaters, they share a friendship enriched by mutual respect and strengthened by their transparency with each other. That friendship adds vibrant color to their lives both on and off the ice.

LEFT WITH A CHOICE

There are many possible reactions to the disappointment that accompanies an injustice. Some people choose to focus on the past and the letdown of their losses. This fosters bitterness, an acid that eats away at their very nature.

Others blame God for the unfortunate circumstances they encounter in life. This builds a wall between them and the One who can heal their heartache. They think of Him as a president who signs and vetoes bills, examining each potential natural occurrence to see if it has use or purpose. Then He either makes it happen or vetoes it by divine intervention.

Unfortunately, one of the common platitudes offered by those trying to console the person knocked down by an injustice is, "God has a purpose for all of this." They assume God inflicts inequitable situations in order to prepare a person for a greater mission in life. The injured athlete is to look at his or her pain as an opportunity sent by God to become more mature and full of faith; he is often encouraged to think that God must really know he has stamina and is therefore being put through this.

There are a couple of questions this viewpoint raises: If God is in fact the One inflicting the injustice to cause maturity in our lives, how can we go to Him for help? In other words, if He is the source of our pain, how could we go to Him for comfort? We couldn't! Only a sadistic God would impose pain and then say, "Let me nurse your wounds and heal your pain."

The belief that God initiates injustice assumes He sometimes operates contrary to His nature. Scripture tells us that God is a just, fair, kind, and loving Father. Would a loving earthly father purposely inflict an injury on his child and then say, "Come here, let me comfort you and help you in your sorrow"? The thought is ridiculous. Neither would a loving and perfect heavenly Father act in this manner.

Scripture says that God did not create man as a

mechanically operated robot to jump at His commands. Instead, we are all designed as unique individuals with the freedom to make our own decisions.

This freedom carries implications: If we make a poor decision, there is a good chance our choice will affect not only us but others, too. Or if we push ourselves too hard, eat junk food, and cut back on sleep, there is a good chance we'll get sick.

When God granted us the freedom of choice, it meant He had to permit us to reap the natural consequences of our choices; otherwise choice would not exist. In order to be consistent with His character, He must allow the principle of cause and effect—a principle He created—to operate.

One of the implications of living in an imperfect world is that we will feel heartache and disappointment. But the bumps and bruises and injustices we encounter aren't necessarily a message from God to shape up. Much tribulation comes simply as a natural consequence of living in a less-than-ideal world.

Christ said, "In the world you have tribulation, but . . . I have overcome the world" (John 16:33 NAS).

God knew we would experience the sting of injustice. With that understanding, He offers the encouraging words that He has overcome the world. As we reach out to Him, His Spirit rises up strong within us and helps us stand on our feet again. He brings peace to our turmoil. He brings order to our chaos. He brings hope to our despair and helps us look forward to bright tomorrows.

When the ax fell, cutting me from the European tour team, I realized, as I nursed my grudges, that I was the only one who really suffered. Blaming God or anyone else didn't help. Hanging on to anger and disappointment was like holding a hot coal in my hand. I was the one getting burned.

No, I didn't go to Europe in 1971. But the summer became a time for me to reevaluate. And in an arena of quiet solitude, I became aware that my disappointment carried a beautiful gift in its hands. Being bumped from the team made me stop and think. As I took time out and pulled away from the demands of my gymnastics life, I had a chance to evaluate objectively.

I realize now that it was during that time of quiet contemplation when God helped me focus my thoughts and clarify my deepest desires. And that was my special gift wrapped in "struggle" paper. As a result, my commitment to gymnastics intensified. With a single-minded purpose I stopped dwelling on the injustice of the past and set my sights for the Olympic Games one year later.

Can anything good come from injustice? Several individuals have answered that question. Sue Soffe discovered an exciting new career. Debbie Landreth Brown gained a perspective on life's hardships that strengthened her character and added a unique sensitivity to her coaching career. Tai and Randy found their friendship enhanced and their appreciation for previous accomplishments broadened. I developed an understanding of the importance of evaluation and quiet contemplation that resulted in a renewed enthusiasm for my goals. And I also learned that when I struggle with life's injustices, I have a choice: I can blame God and lock myself into pain, or call upon Him to heal my heart and help me find the positive hidden in the negative.

THREE

FORGING THROUGH FLUBS AND FEAR

IT WAS ONE year before the 1972 Olympic Games. A stubborn determination fueled my commitment to gymnastics. I had made a resolution to prove to myself, the officials, coaches, and other athletes that I was good enough to represent the United States of America in Munich. Nothing was going to keep me off the team!

During the months prior to the final trials, I was consumed by my commitment to concentrated training, and I made many sacrifices in order to train for competition. As a result, my ninth-grade year wasn't the typical junior high experience most teenagers enjoy. Days were long and demanding. The junior high school principal gave me permission to come to school late so I could train in the gym from 6:00 to 8:30 A.M. After a full day of classes I rushed home to catch a forty-minute nap before practice. By 5:00 P.M. I was back in the gym for six more hours of sweat and strain, pushing my body to the limit. The routines demanded every ounce of grit I could muster. At times the physical exhaustion was overwhelming, but mentally I was alert. Emotionally I was energized. I was compelled to see my dream come true.

As a young girl I had fantasized about making the Olympic team. *Could it ever really happen to me?* I wondered, facing the competition that would make or break my chance of becoming an Olympian.

I was up against the best. Going into the final trials, most critics in the sports world saw the first five spots on the team locked up. The real competition was for the sixth spot. Earlier in the year, I placed seventh at the first elimination meet and fourth at the semifinal trials, so I knew I had a good crack at making the team. But so did seven other gymnasts. All my hopes and dreams hung in the balance as I faced the third and deciding meet.

The final trials consisted of four grueling days of hard competition. All the athletes were judged on two rounds of compulsories and two rounds of optionals. (Most meets are only one round of each). This tested our consistency in performance.

My first rotation was on the vault. I did fairly well; nothing exceptional, but no major errors. After the vault, I was in fourth place. The compulsory bars came next. Compulsories are not created to be difficult. They are designed to challenge athletes to perform simple skills as close to perfection as possible.

I felt fantastic through the first part of the routine, but then it happened. I swung around to grab the high bar, and it wasn't there. Before I knew it, I had landed with a thud, flat on the mat under the bars. At that time, a full point was deducted for a fall. In a sport that is judged by hundredths of a point, a fall is a major setback.

In a foggy daze, I remounted the bars to finish my routine. I could not believe I had lost control on such a simple element. I was numb. Convinced that I had aced myself out of the competition, I mentally threw in the towel. My scores confirmed the nightmare. After the first two rotations I was in twenty-ninth place out of thirty competitors.

In between sessions, I put on my warm-ups and took a long, lonely walk back to the hotel. I cried the whole way. I felt so empty . . . all those hours, all those years, all those dreams, and it was such a simple move. I had done it hundreds of times in practice. If only I could do it over again.

Although I was only fourteen at the time of this competition, it seemed as if it had been years since I decided to train for the Olympics. Heading toward the hotel, I found myself overshadowed by a cloud of failure. Nowhere in my deepest feelings was there the instinct to fight back. Tears of insecurity blurred my vision as I compared my low standing to the challenge of making the Olympic team. I no longer saw clearly enough to navigate toward my goal.

I walked into the hotel room in a stupor, ready to abandon my dreams. My roommate, Linda Metheny, sensed something was wrong and asked sympathetically, "How did your routines go?" All I could mumble through my sobbing was, "I fell off." She hugged me and tried her best to speak words of encouragement.

Later, Dick came to the room for one of his father-daughterlike talks. With compassion in his eyes, he said, "Nancy, I've seen other athletes fall off the bars in competition and still fight their way back to the top. If you want it badly enough, I know you can do it! You just have to pull yourself together and get back out there and fight."

Dick's words were more than mere encouragement. They acted as a beacon piercing the dense fog of failure engulfing my spirit. His advice resurrected my dream and made me realize I could press on toward my goal.

It was a long four days of competition. Slowly I crept back. With each routine, my score moved me up a place or two. Going into the final two events I was tied with Debbie Hill for the sixth spot on the Olympic team. Even though the top seven athletes were designated

Olympians, only the top six would compete in Munich. The seventh gymnast was the alternate. Technically, I was vying for the chance to compete in the Olympic Games. I knew I had to get a 9.3 or better on my final floor exercise in order to beat Debbie's marks.

I was sure I could achieve that score. Yet, warming up in the corner of the arena, visions of a major stumble during my dance moves challenged my confidence. Mentally, I wrestled with the fear of failing and blowing my one last chance to become an Olympian. So, behind the bleachers at the Anaheim Convention Center, I took a moment to call on the one Source who could pin that fear to the mat. I asked God to calm my anxiety and help me perform my best. In the short time it took to whisper that prayer, tension gave way to self-assurance.

The green flag was raised and I started my performance. Adrenaline pumped through my body and I had no problem completing the tumbling passes. I finished the routine, sensing it was one of the best I had ever performed.

I left the mat huffing and puffing, dying to see my marks and yet afraid to look up at the score cards. It seemed like hours before the judges were ready to reveal my score. Then the numbers flashed up: 9.5! I had done it! My heart raced with exhilaration. Dick grabbed me and swung me around. My family and friends were jumping up and down screaming. In a swirl of excitement I kept saying to myself, *I did it!* . . . *I did it!* I had to convince myself that my dream really had come true. It didn't seem possible, for just three days earlier I was ready to throw in the towel.

As I made that lonely walk back to my hotel room after the first day of competition, forward momentum toward my goal had been halted by a humiliating mistake. I had lost sight of my dream. As I dwelled on the stupid blunder I made on the bars, my natural reaction was to quit. I was ready to give up, but Dick's advice brought my hopes back to life and helped me refocus on my goal.

The next few days taught me that I don't have to be intimidated by failure because failure can be temporary. I was convinced when I fell off the bars that my mistake meant an automatic exit off the track to success. I was certain my dreams had come to a crashing halt. But now I see more clearly. I realize that my error was just one small piece of the puzzle—not the completed picture.

BLOOPS AND BLUNDERS

Do you ever feel overwhelmed by mistakes? Are there times when you feel you're bumbling through life with two left feet? Have you ever been convinced that you are the sum total of a long list of bloops and blunders? During times like these, it is easy to lose sight of your goals. Tunnel vision sets in as you magnify your inadequacies and ignore your strengths.

Failure is, without a doubt, one of the most difficult hurdles along life's path. Mistakes block our vision, drain us of enthusiasm, and threaten our confidence. Wrong steps, miscalculated figures, ill-timed words, and halfhearted efforts often serve to bump us off the track leading to our goals.

Unfortunately, this obstacle called failure accosts everyone at one time or another because no one is perfect. Failure is unavoidable. If you are like most people, one small mistake and, *wham!* You're rendered helpless by the fear of failing again.

If failure is such a common nemesis to those pursuing excellence, how can we deal with errors and inadequacies and find the courage to pick ourselves up after stumbling? How can we regain forward momentum? Can anything good come from blundering?

Yes. The record books prove that many people with celebrated success stories at some point struggled with failing, and the resultant fear of failing again.

A USEFUL TOOL FOR WYOMIA TYUS

In 1964, a nineteen-year-old track-and-field athlete from Griffin, Georgia, surprised herself and the world by winning the gold medal in the women's one-hundred-meter dash at the Olympic Games in Tokyo, Japan. After returning home from the Orient, four long years of competition separated Wyomia Tyus from the 1968 Olympic Games and the possibility of becoming the first track-and-field athlete, male or female, to win back-to-back one-hundred-meter events. She was immediately thrust into the limelight that often accompanies a gold medalist. Introduced at the start of the races as, "the current Olympic Champion," Wyomia battled the fear of failure. After all, how long can one person continue giving the best performance in the world?

Fortunately, Wyomia's coach at Tennessee State University, the legendary Ed Temple, was able to help her keep things in perspective. She says, "Ed used to tell us, what might seem to be a failure on a given day, if analyzed properly, can be used to make you a better athlete and a better person."

Coach Temple helped his athletes learn from their mistakes so they would continue to progress despite failure. His long-term perspective snatched them out of the emotional ruins of shortsightedness.

Wyomia learned to view failure from an analytical perspective. She responded to setbacks with evaluation. When she faltered in her performance, she took a mental step back and analyzed the situation.

Wyomia says, "When I lost a race, I asked myself, *What could I have done differently? Did I prepare properly? How can I make adjustments so that this doesn't happen again?*" As she went back to workouts and focused on strengthening her weaknesses, failure evolved from an ugly monster into a useful tool.

As Wyomia focused on the facts, she minimized the negative effects of failure. The temptation to dwell on past mistakes lost its grip. Rather than beating herself down for mistakes, Wyomia chose to play the role of an objective bystander and analyze her own performance. With forthright conviction, she harnessed her thoughts and concentrated on what she needed to do to win.

Her strategy worked. Stepping up to the starting blocks in the 1968 Olympic Games in Mexico City, she was unencumbered by memories of past losses, and energized by the knowledge that she was prepared to win the race. On that rainy day in October, Wyomia Tyus stole all the thunder as the first to hit the tape after sprinting one hundred meters in a world record time of eleven seconds. In addition to being the fastest woman runner in the world, she accomplished a feat that hasn't been duplicated by any other athlete: two successive Olympic gold medals in the one-hundred-meter dash.

Part of Wyomia's success came from learning to view her failures as opportunities for improvement. Losses became valuable lessons that only enhanced her athletic career. Another two-time Olympian, Kathy Johnson, also discovered a nugget of truth about failure during the challenges along her pursuit of excellence.

LIFE GOES ON

Known as the "old lady" of gymnastics, Kathy Johnson had an illustrious eight-year career on the U.S. national team. In many sports, eight years of national and international participation is average for an athlete. But gymnastics is a sport for youngsters. It is highly unusual to find anyone at a major international women's gymnastics meet over the age of eighteen. Kathy bypassed the statistics and competed in the 1984 Olympics at the seasoned age of twenty-four!

Having had such a long tenure in the sport, she walked the comeback trail more than once. Due to several injuries and subpar performances, Kathy faced difficult questions from sports enthusiasts. Could she make it to the top one more time? Would her body be able to handle the challenge, at her age? Hadn't she sacrificed enough already? Haunted by mistakes of the past, she also questioned her future in the sport.

Today, Kathy says she learned how to persevere. "The greatest lesson I learned from the low points of my athletic career was that life goes on after a loss. A fall does not mean the world will end."

Kathy recalls one competition when she walked away dejected after a disappointing fall in her uneven bar routine. "As soon as I left the mats, I glanced back and noticed the next performer's coach run in to quickly prepare the bar setting for his athlete. I saw the girl standing over the chalk box, nervously preparing to compete. The judges finished computing my score and were ready to evaluate the next routine. In the midst of all the hubbub, a profound truth hit me. The world did not stop when I fell off the bars. My mistake, while affecting my place in the standings, was not as life-altering as I made it out to be."

Kathy Johnson's long career on the U.S. national team was not without frustration and embarrassment.

Bogged down by the fear of failure, there were times when her main goal shifted from winning a medal to finishing a competition without any major bobbles. And yet, she always managed to qualify for the most important and prestigious events each year.

How was she able to pick herself up so many times? What secrets enabled her to overcome her fear? Part of her strength came from leaving the ghosts of past failures behind her: "Once a competition was over, there wasn't anything I could do to change my earlier performance. I became my own worst enemy when I catastrophized my blunders. So I fought hard to control my thoughts. Whenever visions of a bad fall dashed across my mind during practice, I pictured them as ghosts from the past that served no constructive purpose in my training, and I determined to leave those ghosts sitting in the bleachers at my last competition. I tried to approach each workout and meet with a clean slate."

And what was the result of Kathy's mental self-control? She whipped the fear of failure and qualified for more major U.S. national teams (Olympic and World Championship) than any gymnast in the history of the sport. Her career was highlighted by two Olympic and two World Championship medals, and eight National Championships. More important, Kathy earned the respect of coaches and athletes worldwide because of her determination to persevere despite failure.

THERE IS HOPE!

While failure and the resulting fear of future failure may seem like an impossible hurdle to overcome, it is not. We can learn to work our way past fear rather than allowing it to be a barrier to our success.

Fear becomes more manageable when we realize that as long as we continue to grow, we will experience fear of failing. It never goes away when we're taking risks and striving toward our dreams. Anxiety will be our sidekick when we forge through unknown territory.

We are not the only ones to feel fear when taking on a new challenge. All the people we admire because of their ability to overcome past failures still experience fear, just as we do. They aren't immune to all-encompassing anxiety. But they transform it into a companion that accompanies them in their adventures, rather than allowing it to be an anchor that holds them fixed in one spot. They have learned to live with fear, and keep plodding forward.

One way to conquer the fear of doing something is to *do it*. The "doing it" comes *before* the fear goes away, not vice versa. Anxiety doesn't automatically diminish, but attempting the very thing we are afraid of usually calms our fears because feelings follow actions.

But what if you are completely paralyzed by fear and unable to act? What if fear has you by the tail, and you just can't seem to break loose? Perhaps you fall into the trap of forgetting that you're a four-dimensional person living in a three-dimensional world. You are more than a package of body, intellect, and emotions. You are a spiritual being, too. And there are times when you face challenges beyond your own natural abilities, and you need supernatural help to clear this hurdle called fear.

The Bible tells us that God does not give us a spirit of fear, but of power, love, and sound judgment. When your own resources are drained, God's unlimited reserve of power, love, and sound judgment are available. You may not be able to shake loose the fear that has you bound, but He can. That's why He bids you not to be "anxious about anything, but in everything, by prayer and petition, with thanksgiving, present your requests to God. And the peace of God, which transcends all understanding, will guard your hearts and your minds in Christ Jesus" (Philippians 4:6, 7 NIV).

No, successful people are not immune to hardships, mistakes, or the ensuing fear of failure. They view these things as a reality of life and a built-in part of their travel—not a permanent exit off the road to excellence, but a temporary detour. Like Wyomia Tyus, they see mistakes as an opportunity for improvement. Like Kathy Johnson, they minimize the negative effects of failure by abandoning thoughts of past mistakes and facing new challenges with a clean slate of hope and confidence. They realize life goes on after a blunder. And one failure is only one piece of the puzzle, not the completed picture.

Many call on God to help them move forward when

the fear of failure is all-consuming. While persevering, stability is driven deeply into their personality. A serendipity to all of this is that in the process, more often than not, their hope is restored and their dreams become reality. Perhaps this is what the Apostle Paul had in mind when he said:

> *We exult in our tribulations, knowing that tribulation brings about perseverance, and perseverance, proven character, and proven character, hope. And hope does not disappoint us, because God has poured out his love into our hearts by the Holy Spirit, whom he has given us.*
>
> *See Romans 5:3, 4* NAS

FOUR

ESCAPING THE EVILS OF ENVY

ENVY. IN OUR competitive world, it's almost impossible not to compare ourselves with others. The talents, possessions, personalities, honors, and abilities of others lure us into a comparison game. Once caught in this trap, we can become sidetracked in our own pursuit of excellence. Progress comes to a screeching halt when we are consumed with thoughts of what we don't have, where we fall short, or when we are due credit we don't receive.

I must confess that there were times during my gymnastics career when I felt overwhelmed with envy.

One example revolved around a balance beam stunt I learned for the '72 Olympics.

A new trend at that time was to use tumbling stunts as a part of balance beam routines. Aerial work (tumbling without hands touching the beam) had never been done in the Olympics. My coach helped me learn an aerial back somersault on the beam, a trick that would be unique if I perfected it. A great deal of my time at the Olympic training camp at Yale University was spent working on this trick. Successfully performing the aerial back "somie" in Munich would open the eyes of the judges and give me needed credibility.

Training to perfect this move took its toll on my body. Each back somersault jammed the balls and heels of my feet onto the hard wooden beam. (Until 1976, the balance beam was not padded as it is now.) I must have done fifty somies per day.

When practices wound down at the end of the day, my feet felt as if concrete blocks had been dropped on them. I actually had secret thoughts of crawling back to my room. At night I soaked my feet in a hot bubbling whirlpool while I nursed the blisters on my hands in buckets of ice. As I sat, sprawled out on a chair with my feet in the whirlpool and my hands in ice cubes, a thousand miles away from my family, it was hard for my fifteen-year-old mind to jump with joy over being an Olympic athlete!

Prior to leaving for Munich, the team spent a week of intense training in Washington, D.C. We were outfitted in official Olympic uniforms and met our U.S. team-mates from other sports. Our stay concluded with a visit to the White House and an official send-off banquet with Vice President Spiro Agnew.

Once in Munich, the pace quickened as we prepared for our performances and I continued to perfect my somie. Finally our first day of competition arrived. My stomach churned with nervous excitement as I did the finishing touches on my hair and makeup. In a few short moments we lined up according to height in the tunnel leading into the competition hall.

The atmosphere inside the arena was unlike anything I had experienced. The air was electric and filled with a majestic marching song exploding through the loud-speakers. The huge Sporthalle, decorated in vivid pastel colors, came alive as the fanfare of Olympic competition began. Officials wearing bright green uniforms hustled everywhere, attending to their business. Spectators and the press eagerly waited for the athletes to begin competition.

Our time had finally come! We marched into the Sporthalle behind the USA placard along with teams from Great Britain, France, and the Netherlands. I felt patriotic as we were led around the arena to our first event. Flag-waving spectators erupted in unison, yell-ing, "U-S-A! U-S-A!" I realized the awesome responsi-bility of competing for an entire nation. Pride swelled within me for the letters I wore on my back and the country I represented.

The opening march ended and we hurried to the podium for our three-minute warm-up. There was so little time to prepare. Now I understood why the coaches relentlessly drove us at training camp. Our performance had to be second nature. There was no place for lack of confidence or for worry. Now it was time to compete in the Olympic Games.

The first day of competition was the compulsory round. Our goal was to execute the required routines as cleanly as possible. I completed all four performances without any major mistakes. After the compulsories we were in fifth place as a team, only three-tenths out of third place, which would mean a team medal. We were pleased with our efforts, but we were not pleased with our scores and knew we had to work hard to move up in the standings. The next day we headed into the Sporthalle once again for the optional competition with high hopes of a best-ever finish for the American team.

Eyes from all over the world were upon us. I realized immediately why Dick had put so much emphasis on perfecting my beam routine. The initial event in the optional round was the balance beam, and I was first. My shoulders felt heavy with the responsibility to set the pace for the rest of my teammates.

The official flashed my number. I was up. The aerial back somersault in the middle of the routine worried me the most, but I felt fairly secure as I mounted the beam. Concentrating on each intricate move, I completed the back somie with only a slight wobble. But I stayed on the beam.

I heard my family and friends across the arena cheer with rip-roaring applause and I remember thinking, *I just completed the first aerial back somersault ever performed in the Olympic Games!*

It was an effort to bring my concentration back to the routine when my emotions were flying around inside like helium balloons with the knots untied. But I couldn't let my mind wander for one split second. I recentered my attention and continued.

The rest of the routine went smoothly. I dismounted with a smile that reached from ear to ear. I knew I had just accomplished one of the most important goals in my life. Invigorated by the lively crowds and a deep sense of achievement, I floated back to my seat on the sidelines.

After the six of us had competed on the beam, we moved on to the floor exercise, the vault, and finally, the uneven bars. As each routine was completed, our scores indicated we had a chance to improve on our fifth-place standing. We were optimistic about moving up in the ranks. The rest of the meet passed quickly. Just one hour later we marched out of the arena realizing that, yes, we had given the competition our best shot. When all the scores were tallied, the U.S. women's team finished fourth, which was the highest ranking ever received by an American women's gymnastics team.[1]

In the days that followed, I experienced a vast array of emotions. I was deeply satisfied with my performance and felt a great sense of accomplishment. We had not won the bronze medal but we had made tremendous strides to finish in fourth place. The international gymnastics community agreed that the American women were indeed among the best in the world. I had played a part in that team effort. Individually, I had been the first person in the world to perform the aerial back somersault on the balance beam in Olympic competition. It was the beginning of a whole new era for the sport, and I had contributed to that change.

But I was disappointed when many of my efforts went unnoticed. After our competition was over, we attended a dinner hosted by the United States Gymnastics Federation to recognize our accomplishments. I embarrassed myself with tears of envy as I watched my five teammates proudly receive an international award for placing among the top thirty-six competitors. All of them were recognized by the national officials for their outstanding performances. All I got was a pat on the back even though I was tied for thirty-seventh place, only one-tenth of a point away from the top thirty-six.

I kept thinking, *If only I had pointed my toes a little harder. If only I had been placed second or third in the lineup, perhaps my scores would have been higher. If only I were a better gymnast. If only I had blonde hair and pigtails! If only . . . if only. . . .*

The kind words of Jackie Fie, the U.S. judge and

representative on the International Technical Committee, pulled me out of the clouds of frustration and helped me regain my perspective. With a big hug, she reassured me: "Your contribution was just as important as everyone else's. Remember, Nancy, this was your first international meet, and you have a very promising future." Her eyes sparkled with sincerity. I appreciated her sensitivity at a time when I felt extremely left out and insignificant.

When the Games ended I looked forward to viewing tapes of the television coverage of our competition and to hearing the impressions of my family and friends who were not in Munich. But when I got home I found out that they had not seen much of me on TV and had to rely mostly on newspaper accounts of what I had done. My grandparents spoke of their frustrations. They saw me mount the podium to perform. Then the camera switched to coverage of another sport. Some of my friends at school wondered if I had even competed. Very little credit was given to the incredible improvement made by the entire team.

Most of the television coverage centered on a four-foot, ten-inch Russian pixie by the name of Olga Korbut. She managed to steal the hearts of millions with her spectacular moves and vivacious personality. Olga Korbut and ABC made gymnastics a spectator sport, bringing drama, excitement, and emotion into millions of living rooms across the country. The American public became personally involved with this young woman's quest for the gold.

I had to swallow my pride several times during the following year when Olga's Olympic performance on the balance beam was continually replayed on television and recalled in newspapers. She also had performed an aerial back somersault on the beam. Since most eyes were glued to her every movement, very few saw me perform the same stunt at the Olympics several hours earlier. Hence, Olga was mistakenly credited as being the first person to execute that move on the balance beam in the Olympic Games.

When I won the National Balance Beam Championship the following year, a newspaper account described my routine: "She completed a back somersault. It was fluid—almost as if it had not been less than a year since Russia's Olga Korbut laid it on the judges for the first time last September in Munich."[2]

My first reaction after reading this account was to call the reporter and set him straight on his Olympic facts. With a strong sense of injustice, I longed for the credit due my accomplishment. But realizing the futility of such a call, I swallowed my pride and chalked up another point for the Olga Korbut craze!

Unlike Olga, I did not win any medals in the Olympic Games. But when I finished my last routine in the competition, I was confident that I had tasted success. Yet my accomplishments seemed relatively insignificant. Had I been unrealistic in assessing my abilities?

Were my achievements something I fabricated in my mind to justify the importance of my efforts? These questions surfaced as I pondered my participation in the Olympic Games. My fifteen-year-old mind didn't have the answers.

As I sat at the awards banquet shortly after the Olympics, I knew I had made some significant accomplishments, but the desire for more recognition robbed me of contentment. When others received honor, I longed for credit, too. Envy overpowered my sense of inner peace.

As I reflect on my own frustrations during this time, I realize that struggles like these are not uncommon among those pursuing excellence. It is humbling to take a backseat when others are honored. It is easy to feel left out when credit due is snatched away by someone else, especially when it is someone in the limelight. Disappointment can overshadow even those with a seemingly unlimited amount of self-assurance.

What are we to do with feelings of envy? How can we deal with the frustration that swells inside when we deserve credit, but no praise is given?

Hindsight provides valuable perspective as I grapple with these questions. Several Olympiads have passed since 1972. My Olympic performance has joined the ranks of the many athletes who competed before me. Our team accomplishments have been overshadowed by the talents, personalities, and performances of those who followed us. The new stunts we performed in 1972 are commonplace today. Olga Korbut has been replaced by Nadia Comaneci and then Mary Lou Retton as the queen of gymnastics.

The evidence is overwhelming: The reward of recognition is temporary at best. Years later, the awards and accolades I did receive are in my scrapbooks as wonderful mementos of a special time in my life. Today, as a wife, mother, and businesswoman, it is not so much past accomplishments that influence my identity as the lessons gleaned from relationships during my Olympic years.

From the circumstances surrounding my back somersault, I learned the danger of sizing up my efforts against the accomplishments of others. Comparison is a weed that chokes the roots of contentment and kills satisfaction. Why? Because there will always be someone who has the ability to achieve greater feats and more polished stunts.

I had to learn to quit playing the comparison game. Esteeming the admirable qualities in my rivals seemed to help. I looked for their attractive characteristics. I searched for ways to learn from them. In a sense, their outstanding features became qualities for me to aim toward rather than a ruler for measurement against my shortcomings.

I also found that envy disappeared when I made an effort to understand the people who overshadowed me. It has been said that we can never dislike anyone we really know.

Several years after the Olympics, the Soviet national team (led by Olga Korbut) and the U.S. national team (of which I was a member) spent two weeks performing together at the World's Fair in Spokane, Washington. Since this was not a competitive affair, we all relaxed and enjoyed one another. One day after a shopping spree, my roommates and I invited everyone to our room to show off our purchases. In the middle of July, Olga pranced into the room with her head held high, stylishly modeling a big furry winter coat. She was bursting with pride over what she called her "bargain."

Then someone came up with the brilliant idea that we should teach our Russian counterparts how to blow bubbles with bubble gum. I'll never forget the reflection of eight giggling girls crowding around the mirror, hilariously cheering for each bubble blown. With the help of a silly little stick of chewing gum, we managed to overcome our national differences. In spite of a language barrier, we began relating to one another as real people, with emotions and personalities. This experience helped me to see Olga in a new light. As I developed a casual friendship with her, my envy began to subside.

ALWAYS A BRIDESMAID

No one watching the 1976 Olympics will ever forget the name of the petite Romanian dynamo who received the first perfect score in Olympic gymnastics history.

After her compulsory uneven bar routine, the name *Nadia*, like the number ten, became synonymous with perfection. The judges and audience alike were spell-bound by Nadia Comaneci's daring routines and precise technique. She set the standard for which all other gymnasts would strive.

But few will remember the name of the gymnast Nadia claimed was her fiercest competitor. Teodora Ungureanu received the next best score to perfection (9.95) on several occasions and finished only a fraction of a point behind Nadia at those Games. Were it not for a bout with the flu, Teodora might have been the Romanian sensation who rocked the gymnastics world. Their coach, Bela Karolyi, remembers the circumstances:

In 1975, I received permission from the Romanian Gymnastics Federation to hold tryouts to choose one junior girl to compete at the 1975 European Champion-ships in Skien, Norway. My wife, Marta, and I had a large crop of youngsters, including Nadia and Teodora, training with us in Onesti. All were exceptional athletes and equally talented.

Teodora was very close to my heart. She was so full of life, always smiling, and such a pleasure to coach. During the last workout before the trials, I secretly pulled for her. She had won most competitions up to that point and looked like she would easily win the upcoming meet. I even started getting her travel ar-rangements in order.

On the day of competition, I noticed that her eyes

were red, and she wasn't her usual chipper self. After taking her temperature, we realized she was suffering with a bad case of the flu. But she had to compete if she wanted to qualify for the national team. Teodora made it through the meet, but fell off the balance beam during her routine.

In the end, Nadia Comaneci won the trials and made her debut in Skien by winning four individual medals and handing the Russian gymnastics star, Ludmilla Touresheva, her first major loss. That competition established a reputation for Nadia that made her unbeatable in the 1976 Olympics.

One of the most painful memories I have as a coach is that Teodora, one of my favorite gymnasts, never received the full recognition she deserved.

Had Teodora Ungureanu competed at any other time in gymnastics history, she undoubtedly would have been crowned queen of the sport. She performed many of the same daring moves as Nadia and executed her routines with style that outclassed most of her competitors. Yet time and again that first-place honor was bestowed upon her teammate. Teodora and many other athletes were forced to compete in the shadow of the great Nadia Comaneci.

No doubt Teodora spent many intense moments in soul-searching, wishing circumstances were different. Karolyi says, "I know Teodora experienced great emotional pain seeing Nadia receive all of the honor and recognition."

Yet despite their competitive rivalry, Teodora was always the first to offer Nadia words of encouragement and support. Karolyi remembers, "Teodora was known as the motivator of the team, who constantly cheered for everybody else and unselfishly helped others." Even the videotape of the 1976 Olympic routines displays the enthusiastic congratulations Teodora offered Nadia after her performances.

What helped Teodora set aside envy? How was she able to enjoy the company of a person of comparable talent who consistently placed higher than she in the standings?

Karolyi claims Teodora simply made a deliberate choice to get the most out of life by rejoicing with her competitors and encouraging them when they excelled. "She had such a zest for life, gymnastics, and people." Even in the sports arena she allowed love to overpower envy.

THERE IS PEACE IN PREFERRING OTHERS

Are there individuals on your team or opponents from other groups whom you would like to snuff out of competition? Do you find yourself overwhelmed with negative emotions when others get the credit you want or deserve? Is it difficult for you to avoid comparing your efforts with those of others?

Most of us have experienced the humbling process of

stepping aside while others receive attention. Perhaps you are a team member whose efforts are overshadowed by those of more visible teammates. Maybe you have watched others receive the glory of winning a trophy, while your performance placed you as an "also ran." Although envy is a common response in a competitive world, it drains energy that can be better used in other areas of life.

God encourages us to have a different response when we are tempted to envy: "Be devoted to one another in brotherly love; give preference to one another in honor. . . . Do not be overcome by evil, but overcome evil with good" (Romans 12:10, 21 NAS). As we choose to esteem others with a humble heart, we open the door to blessings in our own life.

Affirming, supporting, and acquainting ourselves with those in the limelight are a few steps we can take to overcome envy. As we show interest in those we envy, outside of the common bonds that brought us together, we begin to see them as valuable people rather than the objects of our turmoil. As we reach out to those who overshadow us, we begin to understand that they are people like us: individuals with strengths to admire and weaknesses to accept.

Everyone loves to receive credit when credit is due. But when praise does not come our way, we can still find satisfaction in knowing we did our best. As seeds of sensitivity, genuine goodwill toward others, and humility take root in the soil of our lives, character is strengthened. Relationships deepen, and it becomes easier to stifle the disharmony caused by envy. As we esteem those who are honored, we grant ourselves the privilege of enjoying the sweet taste of contentment during our personal journey toward excellence.

Tai Babilonia and Randy Gardner. "[We] have a depth and a quality to our friendship that is only there because we've worked through our disappointment together." PHOTO BY MICHAEL A. ROSENBERG.

Left: NCAA Champion Mary Ayotte flying high over the balance beam for Oregon State University. "By the end of my career, I had accomplished much more than I ever thought possible."

Above: Olympian Debbie Land-reth Brown offering encouragement to her athletes as Arizona State University's women's volleyball coach. "The 1980 Olympic boycott taught me that there will always be circumstances over which we have no control." COPYRIGHT BY KEN AKERS, 1987. ALL RIGHTS RESERVED.

Left: World record holder Bonnie Blair. "My goal in every race is to be technically better." CHAMPAIGN-URBANA NEWS GAZETTE.

My 1972 Olympic teammates and me. *(Left to right)* Kim Chase, Debbie Hill, Joan Moore, Roxanne Pierce, Linda Metheny, me, Cathy Rigby. The international gymnastics community agreed that the American women were among the best in the world. PHOTO BY MILTON SMITH.

NBC's Charlie Jones and me in 1977, on the premiere of "NBC Sports-world" from Oviedo, Spain. "Even if I disagree with my critics, I find great satisfaction knowing I made a deliberate move to bridge the gap between us." PHOTO BY NBC SPORTS.

Left: Network television's first female sports broadcaster, Olympic gold medalist Donna de Varona. "I don't shrink from criticism and I don't allow my critics to steal my dreams." © 1987 COPYRIGHT CAPITAL CITIES/ABC, INC.

Below: Having learned to persevere beyond failures, a confident Kathy Johnson leaps to a bronze medal on the balance beam at the 1984 Olympic Games. PHOTO BY DAVE BLACK.

Known for the high priority she places on genuinely caring for others, four-time Olympian Madeline Manning Mims is first to the tape at the 1980 eight-hundred-meter Olympic trials in Eugene, Oregon. PHOTO BY JEFF JOHNSON.

Mary Lou Retton shares her secrets for success with me at the Caesar's Palace Invitational meet, February 1984.

Above right: Swimmer Debbie Meyer in 1967, on her way to becoming the first woman to win three individual Olympic gold medals. "I told myself I was not the first person to endure emotional stress and physical ailments. Hardship is a part of life."

Above left: Sue Soffe displays the beauty of rhythmic gymnastics. "The possibility of new experiences and rewards often follows closely after an injustice." PHOTO BY FRITZ GIESSLER.

Right: Me on the balance beam, competing in my first international dual meet against the Japanese team in 1972. "I started believing that in order to be accepted, I had to make Olympic teams in everything I did."

Right: Olympic figure skater Janet Lynn, "communicating Christ's love to her audience." PHOTO BY MARGARET S. WILLIAMSON.

Below: The "fastest woman runner in the world" in 1964; Wyomia Tyus wins the gold medal in the one-hundred-meter dash at the Tokyo Olympics. "When I lost a race, I asked myself, *What could I have done differently?*"

Above: Fierce competitors and close friends, Romanian gymnastics stars Teodora Ungureanu *(left)* and Nadia Comaneci. PHOTO BY ALLAN BURROWS/ INTERNATIONAL GYMNAST.

Right: From Olympic torchbearer in 1980 to Olympic athlete in 1984, luge sensation Bonny Warner. "It pays to take risks." PHOTO BY U.S. LUGE ASSOCIATION.

FIVE

CONQUERING THE VICTIM MENTALITY

"WHY ME?"

We ask this familiar question when the chips are stacked against us. As circumstances interfere with our preconceived agenda, self-pity stands knocking at the door of our emotions. This "victim mentality" is eager to take up residence in any life tainted by unfulfilled dreams and expectations.

After being the target of sudden, arbitrary, and unpredictable misfortune, most of us suffer psychological consequences. Sidetracked from our pursuit of success by conditions beyond our control, it doesn't take much to convince us that we have been handed a raw deal. Even the strongest sports stars are likely to experience shock, anxiety, depression, and shame when their understanding of how they fit into the world of athletics is shattered.

Many athletes have been knocked down by unfortunate circumstances. Some have had the uncanny ability to bounce back and escape self-pity. Rather than believing everything was a total disaster when the odds were against them, they saw the positive side of their endeavors, too. They realized that not every hour of every day was completely disappointing and without hope. Meet Debbie Meyer and Bonny Warner, women who teach us valuable lessons about sidestepping the victim mentality.

WHEN IT RAINS, IT POURS

Swimmer Debbie Meyer heard the persistent knock of self-pity as she prepared for the 1968 Mexico City Olympics. The favorite in the women's two-hundred-, four-hundred-, and eight-hundred-meter freestyle, Debbie had high hopes of becoming the first woman in Olympic history to win three individual gold medals. But prior to competition, she was a victim of circumstances that threatened this possibility.

For months, a nagging case of bursitis in Debbie's shoulders limited her water training. (Lap workouts are essential to maintain endurance and technique for world-class swimmers.) Debbie knew her chances of winning diminished every day she spent out of the water. Rest was the only prescription for healing her shoulders. Concentrating on dry-land exercises and hoping for the ability to ignore her pain during the Olympics, Debbie prepared for competition.

But Murphy's Law was in operation the day she left for Mexico. Running to a pay phone, Debbie tripped over a curb and twisted her ankle. A visit to the doctor at the Olympic Village medical clinic confirmed that she had a bad sprain. She knew the injury would hamper her ability to push off the starting block as well as the side of the pool. This meant seconds added to her time and the possible loss of medals. Hobbling around on crutches the first several days at the Games, Debbie lived with the turmoil generated by thoughts like, *Of all times to trip! Why now? How could I have done this to myself?*

Debbie also faced other obstacles. Efforts to concentrate in training were threatened by a possible ruling of the U.S. Women's Olympic Swimming Committee to limit the number of events in which a swimmer could compete. Citing the altitude problem and the competition schedule in Mexico City, the committee wanted to prohibit athletes from swimming in both the two-hundred- and eight-hundred-meter freestyle. The final for the two-hundred-meter race was to be held the same day as the preliminaries for the eight-hundred-meter race.

Debbie recalls, "I felt the possible ruling was somewhat politically motivated, authored by coaches of other swimmers who wanted to limit my chances for medals. My feelings were continually in flux. It was hard not to think, *The world is out to get me!* I had to keep my thoughts focused on the preparation needed for each race, instead of ruminating about what might or might not happen." Fortunately, before the team left for Mexico, the committee decided to allow Debbie to compete in all three events.

But the frustrations continued. At 5:30 A.M. on the morning of the "dreaded double," Debbie was awakened by a horrible attack of gastroenteritis, humorously referred to as "Montezuma's Revenge"! Six hours later, five pounds lighter, dehydrated and drained of energy, she stood at the starting blocks for the qualifying heat of the eight-hundred-meter freestyle. *Will I be able to finish the race? Can I muster the energy to compete in the two-hundred finals later today, or will my body betray me?* she questioned.

Debbie could easily have justified a subpar performance. Like annoying pests, the injury, the illness, and the political tension gnawed at her confidence. Yet with courage, she slammed the door on self-pity and rewrote the record books by setting three Olympic records. After winning these three individual Olympic gold medals in 1968, she also became the third woman in the world to receive the Sullivan Award, which honors the U.S. Amateur Athlete of the Year.

What enabled Debbie to avoid the victim mentality?

How did she overcome the temptation to feel sorry for herself with so many strikes against her? She says:

> I reminded myself that I was not the first person to endure emotional stress and physical ailments. Hardship is part of life. I forced myself to focus on performing my best and not to dwell on my misfortune. It would have been easy to justify a halfhearted effort with thoughts like, *I've had so many setbacks . . . I can't possibly achieve my goals.* But I wanted to win, so I convinced myself at the starting blocks that each race deserved my best effort, regardless of how I felt.

Debbie concentrated on her rehearsed game plan. Consequently, her best effort was enough to reach her goals.

AN OLYMPIC TORCHBEARER WITH A DREAM

While glued to my TV set during the 1984 Winter Olympics, I was fascinated by the profile of American athlete Bonny Warner, from Mount Baldy, California. Having fought the effects of asthma as a child, she had every reason to feel like a victim. But Bonny was driven by a dream of becoming an Olympian. At the age of four she took up swimming, running, and bicycling to improve her lung capacity. During high school she was an avid downhill skier, and she also competed in track, cross-country, and field hockey.

In 1979, after graduating from high school, Bonny entered an essay contest to compete for the privilege of representing the state of California as a torchbearer for the 1980 Winter Olympics. Out of six thousand applicants, Bonny won first prize. A portion of her Olympic dream was realized when she carried the flame one leg of its journey to Lake Placid, New York. After fulfilling her torchbearing duties, she followed the flame to the Olympic site and stayed to watch the competition and savor the festive Olympic atmosphere.

Though she didn't see the actual luge competition, Bonny was encouraged by a friend to take part in an informal luge training program to be held immediately following the Games. With a passion for adventure and her competitive instincts piqued by the Olympic festivities, Bonny jumped at the chance to participate.

The luge, a daring sport, couples the athlete with a four-foot-long, forty-four-pound fiberglass sled. Outfitted in skintight plastic suits (to cut down on wind resistance) the lugers lie on their backs and race feetfirst against the clock down tracks of ice between one thousand and twelve hundred meters long. Moving at speeds of up to sixty-five miles per hour, the margin for error is minimal.

After paying her eight-dollar insurance fee, Bonny received a free sled and helmet and said at the end of the two-week course, "This is the sport for me!"[1] But the odds were against her ever becoming an Olympic luge competitor. She needed a training site, a coach, and the money to support her quest.

At about that time, she received word from Levi Strauss and Company that out of 1.8 million entries, her name had been chosen in a drawing to receive a five-thousand-dollar grand prize in their self-help, motivational sweepstakes. The prize was designed to assist people in reaching their potential. Bonny used the money to buy a sled and a plane ticket to Germany so that she could train with and learn from one of the top-ranked luge teams in the world.

She appeared at the German luge track unable to speak the language but with tremendous enthusiasm to learn the sport. She found a job as an au pair (housemaid and baby-sitter), and also volunteered to work the midnight shift servicing the luge track. Within a few weeks the German coaches and athletes adopted her as a pseudomember of their team. Their guidance was the turning point in her career.[2]

After two months, Bonny returned to the United States and qualified for the Junior National Luge Team. Within three years she was America's top women's luger to compete at the 1984 Olympics in Sarejevo, Yugoslavia. Had Bonny not crashed on her third run, she would have finished with one of the top ten scores, an unprecedented accomplishment for U.S. Women's Luge athletes. Despite her misfortune in '84, Bonny remains active in competition.[3]

Some people might view Bonny Warner's good fortune as happenstance. But a close look at her life reveals a valuable secret to her success, one we can all embrace when faced with insurmountable odds: It pays to take risks.

Although Bonny originally had no training site, no knowledge of the sport, and no money, she did not succumb to a victim mentality. Refusing to accept defeat as an option, she diligently searched for sources from which to learn. She studied the steps toward her dream and then moved forward, step by step. Blasting through what most people would consider closed doors, she courageously moved out of her comfort zone.

It wasn't easy for Bonny to show up on the German slopes each day, unfamiliar with the language, people, and sport. Being an unknown and inexperienced outsider can drain confidence and poise from even the most self-assured person. But Bonny Warner chose to take patience and optimism with her to Germany. She understood that the only way to realize her dream was to trade the ease and convenience of home for specialized coaching from the best in the world. She dared to take a risk. In stepping out, she never gave in to victimization, and consequently she became a conquerer.

HISTORY IN THE MAKING—CHINESE STYLE

Self-pity stood knocking at my door in 1973 when a disappointing performance and bizarre circumstances threatened my pride and confidence. At that time, thanks to Olga Korbut and the 1972 Olympic Games, gymnastics had gained tremendous worldwide popularity. This enthusiasm eventually transcended amateur athletics and affected the political arena. In January 1973, President Nixon visited the People's Republic of China. He returned, having made an agreement with Chinese Party Chairman Mao Tse-tung to further understanding between our two countries. One way of accomplishing this goal was to stage athletic exchanges between the national gymnastics teams of each country.

To emphasize the impact of these events, it is important to remember that the Chinese were in the midst of the Cultural Revolution. Their leadership had closed the country to outside visitors and had forbidden their athletic teams to participate in international events. No Chinese athletes had competed internationally since the early '60s. More than just an international competition, it was a major political breakthrough and a milestone in the sporting world when, in May 1973, the Chinese sent men's and women's gymnastics teams to compete against the U.S. national team in New York City.

My best year of competition was 1973. I finished third in the all-around at the U.S. Gymnastics Federation National Championships and won the national balance beam title. I was also chosen as the highest-ranking member of a four-women team to compete against the Chinese at Madison Square Garden.

I had high goals. I wanted to contribute to a team victory and to win the individual all-around title. I was in a perfect position to reach those goals. The top U.S. veterans had retired, which left me as one of four Olympic Team members still in active competition. As the only Olympian at this meet, I was hungry for a gold medal.

But even the best-laid plans are sometimes thwarted. A week before I left for New York, I came down with a bad case of the flu. I dragged myself to workouts, feverish and congested. It was very difficult to complete each routine, and the frustration of my circumstances began to drain my competitive spirit.

I had been on a roll. My performance at the recent National Championships had been right in line with my goals for the year. I felt as if I were riding on the crest of a wave, and the momentum just kept building. After competing with the Chinese, I was looking forward to performing in Bulgaria at an International Invitational. I knew these meets were opportunities for me to establish my reputation as one of America's top gymnasts. I was in great shape and ready to conquer the world. Then came the flu. Hoping for an adrenaline surge during competition, I headed for New York, determined to give it my best shot.

Just before arriving in New York, the Chinese delegation met privately with President Nixon in Washington, D.C. He emphasized the political and historical significance of their tour. I knew this was not an ordinary international dual meet when we were processed by Secret Service men assigned to protect the

Chinese. We wore special buttons to ride the buses to and from workouts and to get onto the hotel floor where the Chinese gymnasts were staying.

There was a tremendous exchange of friendship. Each gathering heightened the anticipation of the up-coming competition. The exhaustive press coverage increased that excitement. With each passing day, I felt stronger and more optimistic about winning the all-around.

On the day of competition, the comradery and competitive spirit among the athletes created a unique atmosphere inside the Garden. While warming up, I felt as if I were attending a gala celebration, not a gymnastics meet. It was obvious that a bipartisan crowd filled the arena. Enthusiastic support was offered to gymnasts from both countries. It was as if the spectators in Madison Square Garden were aware they were part of an historic event.

Once the opening ceremonies concluded, it was time to concentrate on my performance. The first rotation, the vault, passed quickly. When it was over, I was in the running for the all-around, and team scores were close. The next event was the uneven parallel bars. I had some unique stunts in my routine and was eager to do them well. But the uneven bars is an endurance event, and by the end of the routine, my energy ran low. When I did the somersault, which was a part of my dismount, I did not have quite enough stamina to complete it. I landed sitting down on the mat, which resulted in a one-point deduction.

I was so tired and frustrated, I wanted to crawl under the mat and hide. With two more events left, I walked slowly back to my seat, trying hard to forget my bar routine.

Thank goodness the balance beam event was next. I was confident I could redeem myself. Since I was the current national champion, I knew I had a favorable reputation on the beam. I was sure I could bounce back. Unfortunately, my reputation didn't help me stay on the beam. Shortly after mounting, I fell off while performing an aerial back somersault—another embarrassing mistake. As I climbed onto the beam to finish my routine, I faced the stark reality that I was not going to win the meet.

Even though I conceded the all-around title, I still looked forward to the final event, the floor exercise. My routine was choreographed to display all the theatrics and power suggested by my musical accompaniment, the classic theme from *2001: A Space Odyssey*. The *New York Times* described what happened next as "the most dramatic event of the evening."

I positioned myself in my opening pose and waited for the music to begin. (The U.S. team chose to do floor routines to tape-recorded accompaniment.) But all I heard over the sound system was garbled noise. I walked off the mat, assuming the sound man had put the wrong tape in the machine. Since we were alternating performances with the men, the announcer called for the next male competitor to proceed.

After a few minutes, I was cued to try again. I went back out on the mat, only to hear the same muffled sounds as before. I was already disappointed about my performance on the bars and beam. Now this! There I stood, alone in the middle of Madison Square Garden, thousands of eyes staring at me as I faced the prospect of performing my floor exercise routine with no music. That's like eating dry toast—boring and flavorless. I looked questioningly at my parents in the audience, hoping they had an extra copy of my music with them. No such luck. The *Sports Illustrated* account best describes the next few moments:

> There was a foul-up in the music for Nancy Thies' floor exercises. Twice she appeared at center mat to perform, only to have the taped music turn garbled and shrill. At last, after an emergency interpretation, the official traveling pianist for the Red Chinese, a small dignified fellow named Chou Chiasheng, took his place at the keyboard and as Nancy performed her complex routines, he watched carefully and composed an extemporaneous arrangement of western classical music that matched her balletic moves perfectly. It was a magnificent international duet. When it was over, Nancy . . . rushed to plant a pretty kiss upon the beaming cheek of Mr. Chou while the entire Garden audience rose to its feet in exultant applause.[4]

Gordon Maddox, commentating on "ABC's Wide World of Sports," succinctly captured the essence of the moment when he said, "This is unprecedented . . . a gal from Urbana and a man from Peking . . . all of a sudden, they've gotten together."[5]

Those few minutes will forever be etched in my memory as some of the most satisfying moments of my gymnastics tenure. Yet I didn't meet my goals. Was I simply allowing the emotion and drama of the evening to erase my embarrassing mistakes, or could I honestly consider my experience a successful endeavor? What transformed a potentially boring performance into one of the highlights of my career? Why did I feel more like a victor than a victim?

As I flew home from New York, I searched for answers to those questions. I recalled the words of Muriel Grossfeld, our team coach. After the garbled music came through the speakers, she said, "You can do your routine without accompaniment or we can see if the Chinese pianist will improvise for you." Those few words offered hope. Muriel's creative suggestion showed me that, more often than not, several options are available when we're caught in a bind.

Exploring a different option turned a dismal situation into a cherished memory. My duet with the Chinese pianist wove color into the tapestry of my life and taught me about escaping the suffocating grip of self-pity.

ONE OF LIFE'S GREATEST FREEDOMS

Do unfulfilled goals or misfortune ever drain your passion for excellence? Have you been duped into thinking you're a victim in a hole with no way out? Don't fall for that lie. One of the greatest freedoms you have in life is the freedom to choose among options. If you have encountered a setback, dare to see more than the obvious in your undesirable circumstances.

Ask God to help you move beyond your comfort zone. He can give you the courage to risk again because He doesn't see you as a victim. In His eyes, you're a survivor: "You are more than a conquerer through Him Who loved you" (see Romans 8:37 NIV). The key words in that verse are *through Him*. He is ready and willing to help you break free from victim thinking by giving you His perspective of yourself and your circumstances. He is eager to give you strength to get back up again: "Though you may grow weary and tired, and stumble badly, if you ask the Lord for help, you will gain new strength. You will have wings like an eagle and be able to walk and not get tired and run and not become weary" (see Isaiah 40:30, 31 NAS). This is God's promise for you.

Conquerers aren't people who never encounter hardship or never fail. They are people who choose never to quit. They are those who know they can have more, and they refuse to settle for less. Instead of dwelling on

"Why me?" they choose to smile at the future and ask, "What next?"

If you encounter unpredictable misfortune along life's journey, let me encourage you to ignore the persistent knocks of self-pity. Hardship is a normal part of any pursuit of excellence. Minimizing the importance of adversity can help you avoid feeling sorry for yourself. Stepping beyond your comfort zone and taking risks can broaden your world and help you discover new talents and relationships. And when Plan A fails, chances are there is a Plan B close at hand, with the power to turn a bad deal into a priceless memory.

SIX

PUTTING ASIDE PERFECTIONISM

PERFECTION. ACCLAIMED BY society as one quality that ensures success, a premium has been placed on the pursuit of this elusive standard. The goal to be entirely without fault or defect is commonly sought by athletes wishing for a gold medal, businessmen dreaming of million-dollar bank accounts, homemakers desiring an immaculate house and talented children, and students aspiring for a wall of academic awards.

Webster defines *perfectionism* as "a disposition to regard anything short of perfection as unacceptable."[1] It is a philosophy often espoused by high achievers. Sometimes it becomes an obsession. Those living by this standard of success carry a self-inflicted burden. Patience runs thin when imperfections interfere with achievements. Within such rigid guidelines, unfulfilled expectations imply failure.

My desire to be perfect evolved from a need to be accepted and esteemed. Relationships were important to me, yet I was never the outgoing, "life of the party" type. I longed for confidence and the courage to reach out to others in friendship.

In 1972, when I arrived home from Munich, my self-esteem was nurtured by my newly achieved status as an Olympian. My accomplishments brought attention from peers and adults and I have to admit, I secretly enjoyed the limelight.

With all of the media attention, I became aware of a celebrity image attached to my name. Even classmates I didn't know stopped me in the hall, eager to get a firsthand report of Olympic life. I chuckled when one of the more popular boys in school, who never paid any attention to me *before* the Olympics, suddenly started treating me like a good buddy!

Since my Olympic quest was a family affair, my dad and I joined the local banquet circuit sharing the "inside story" of our experience with service clubs and athletic teams. Each speaking engagement was a crash course in the art of public relations. I learned to think and communicate in front of large groups of people and received compliments on my speaking ability. The attention went a long way to fulfill my teenage longings for acceptance. I loved feeling famous.

The Munich Games had been my first major international meet, so I was only beginning my career. I had my eye on the '74 World Championships and the '76 Olympic Games. As my confidence and poise developed, I faced the future with great optimism. I felt good about who I was and where I was headed. My self-esteem was further bolstered by the forecasts of local journalists:

> If you want to get to the top, set your goal at an early age, work hard, and never waver.
> Our community has a 15 year-old gymnastics star who is working on this formula. And I'd wager she will go all the way toward attaining her ambitious objective.
> . . . the determination, diligence, and dedication she has already exemplified should continue to drive Nancy Thies to her goal: competing in the '76 Olympics in Montreal and winning a medal in her competitive sport.
> . . . Her outstanding achievements at age 15 are a great stepping-stone toward her Olympic medal winning goal for the future. I think she'll make it.[2]

Although the lofty predictions were a boost to my ego, I sometimes wondered if the sportswriters were talking about the same Nancy Thies I knew! After all, I had a long way to go before being considered a top contender for an Olympic medal. I was flattered that people placed such confidence in me. I liked being known as a high achiever.

I realize now that the positive feedback was meant for encouragement, but as it continued to pour in, something subtle wove its way into my thoughts. I started believing that in order to be accepted, I had to make "Olympic teams" in everything I did. I had to keep up my image. In every aspect of my life, I felt pressure to excel so I wouldn't topple off the pedestals others had erected for me.

I had a hard time liking myself when I wasn't outstanding, which was most of the time! Aside from my relative expertise in gymnastics, I wasn't very talented in anything else. I couldn't play an instrument or sing with much quality. I had to work for good grades. I was emotional and constantly struggled with my weight. To top it all off, I had acne and big ears!

After the Olympics my need to excel in gymnastics intensified. In 1973 Dick Mulvihill, my coach, moved to Oregon with his wife, my former teammate, Linda Metheny. Together they established the National Academy of Artistic Gymnastics. I remained in Illinois and competed for six months without Dick's guidance. His absence hindered my performances. My routines were similar to those I had used in the Olympics a year earlier. While I was "maintaining," my competitors were learning new stunts and improving their routines. I knew I needed to join Dick and Linda in Oregon if I wanted to do well at the '74 World Championships. In the fall of 1973, I left my family in Illinois and moved to the Northwest.

During my first few months in Oregon, I made great progress in training. My aim was to be the national all-around champion, and I felt I was right on target. I learned new stunts, improved my weaknesses, and lost most of the weight I had gained during the summer. Even though I missed my family, I thoroughly enjoyed the new adventure. The novelty of living away from home added some excitement, too!

The first tangible reward for my hard work came the following March when I was chosen to compete in the Soviet Union at the prestigious Riga Invitational. Only the best gymnasts from each country were sent to this meet. I saw my invitation as a vote of confidence from top sports officials. If I did well in Moscow, where Soviet-bloc judging is noted for its bias against Western competitors, my reputation would be established as a credible, internationally ranked gymnast.

But several weeks prior to the trip the winds of fortune seemed to shift. Although I had worked on exciting new stunts, I wasn't ready to perform them in competition. I had to settle for my old routines, which were less difficult and showed little innovation. I knew the other gymnasts' routines would be of a much higher caliber. I was frustrated that my exercises weren't perfected sooner and embarrassed that I wouldn't have some of the best routines in competition.

My one-dimensional life was also taking a toll on my

emotional stability. I had been away from home for seven months, except for a short trip to Urbana at Christmas. The academy was drastically different from life in Illinois. Since I attended school only four hours a day, I had very little contact with the outside world. Day and night I was surrounded by reminders of the sport. Gymnastics had become all-consuming.

I missed the spirited Thies family dinner conversations. I longed for one of our impromptu sing-alongs when we gathered around my older brother, David, at the piano or guitar. I dreamed of spending a lazy summer evening watching my brother John in a Little League game or my sister Anne in a swim meet. You guessed it: A classic case of homesickness had set in.

I was also fighting a major battle with my weight. I was growing up. My body was maturing, and I couldn't control all of the changes. Each week I tried the newest fad diet, frantically trying to lose a pound or two. One week I tried to live on liquids, mostly soup and diet soda. Then I craved solids and decided to try the no-carbohydrate diet. It didn't work. I barely had enough energy to climb out of bed each morning. Vomiting came next. I downed teaspoons of ipecac (a vomit-inducing medicine) to get rid of most of what I ate. But that backfired, too. Eventually my body became immune to the effects of the syrup. Fortunately, I abandoned that process because it wasn't worth being nauseated all day.

Occasionally I neared my ideal weight, but one trip to

the Dairy Queen and a day off from workouts skyrock-
eted the scales five pounds upward. I spent many
frustrating, tearful nights wondering why life was suddenly so difficult.

Being homesick and overweight hampered my performance in Riga. I would love to forget every detail of
that trip to the Soviet Union. I blew just about every
routine in the competition and spent most of my free
time in a hotel room crying, eating, or dreaming of
Illinois. I scolded myself for failing so miserably and
silently blamed my coaches for not making my career a
priority.

My performances indicated that unless things
changed, I would soon be a candidate for the "over the
hill" gang at age sixteen. I was no longer a girl with a
future. Instead of asking, "What's next for Nancy?"
most people were asking, "What's happening to
Nancy?" My momentum had slowed to a virtual stand-
still.

I felt totally out of control. I had blown my image and
didn't want to go back to the United States and face
anyone. Many of my friends had said they admired my
accomplishments. All I could see were my glaring
weaknesses. I hated revealing my imperfections.

Flying home from Russia, I struggled to make sense
out of everything that had happened in the past few
months. Would I ever get out of this rut? How could I
regain my self-respect? Was it possible to make a

commitment to lofty goals and be free from the pressures of perfectionism?

Needing answers, I stopped off in Illinois before
going back to Oregon. My parents were well aware of
my confused state of mind. Prior to leaving for the
Soviet Union, I had spent hours on the phone with
them trying to understand my feelings.

I walked out of the customs area at the O'Hare
International terminal, drained from the long flight. The
next three hours driving home to Urbana were spent
elaborating the details of my trip. Both my mom and I
cried most of the way home.

Dad was so anxious to get to Urbana and relieve the
tension in the car that he ignored the speed limit.
Flashing red lights and screaming sirens came out of
nowhere. Moments later, a state patrolman handed my
dad a ticket. I've often wondered what the officer
thought when he had to deal with a temperamental
driver and two extremely emotional women. I'm sure
that on his lunch break he told quite a story about a
strange family who sobbed their way through his ticket
writing. We all agreed we'd laugh about that ordeal
someday!

The following days were a welcome reprieve. We had
a few of those energetic dinner conversations I had
missed. It was a ritual for all seven of us to talk about
what we had done during the day. I never realized how
much I enjoyed "reporting in." I visited school with my
sister Susie, and saw many of my friends. It was fun to

catch up on all that had happened during the past months.

The most encouraging moments came the night before I returned to Oregon. My parents had spent the week sifting through my frustrations. This late-night therapy session provided an opportunity for them to offer advice. My dad's words were just what I needed to hear.

"We have allowed you to continue in gymnastics, not because you won meets or came home with trophies, but because your character has been strengthened by the challenges you have faced. The last eight years of your life have been spent working very hard toward your goals. Lately you've sacrificed your security here at home in order to give the World Championships your best shot.

"We want you to know, whatever happens at the trials in September, we are proud of you. Your performance has nothing to do with our estimation of you as a person." Then with a smile, he added, "While your accomplishments give us much to boast about, you need to believe that we are most proud of you as a person, and we love you very much."

As we talked, my burden lifted. Although Mom and Dad's support didn't eliminate all of my frustrations, Dad's counsel helped me see my efforts in a new light. Hidden in his words of affirmation was a principle that became the framework around which I rebuilt my self-confidence. *My accomplishments (or lack of) have noth-*

ing to do with my value as a person. Perfection did not determine my worth. Win or lose in gymnastics, I had my whole life ahead of me. The humiliation I felt in the Russian competition was not the end of the world. I returned to Oregon with a new perspective, confident that the people who really mattered to me still loved, accepted, and admired me.

During the following months I also found relief in outside interests. A wonderful couple whose daughter was a gymnast at the academy unofficially adopted me into their family. Wayne and Darlene Hill sensed the pressure I felt and invited me to their home for meals. I spent most weekends with them. Whenever I could get away from the gym, they included me on their mini camping and boating retreats to the nearby Cascade Mountains.

I loved playing the part of a big sister to their children. Eleven-year-old Lori and I went shopping and took long walks together. Eight-year-old Nathan couldn't wait to introduce me to his newest pets (snakes and skunks were his favorites!). Wayne and Darlene treated me as if I were their daughter. Darlene helped sew my leotards, and Wayne's dry sense of humor put the gym chaos in the right perspective. My world was broadened by their family activities. The security I felt in their home went a long way to ease the pain of being away from my own family.

The Hills gave me a gift I will always treasure. It was the gift of balance. With my athletic pursuits as the central focus of my life, I needed outside interests to enlarge my view. Bothersome worries about gymnastics were stilled by the breathtaking scenery of the Pacific Northwest and lively conversations with Wayne and Darlene (about anything but the gym!). The love Lori and Nathan freely gave me recharged my batteries and reminded me there was more to life than wooden beams and dance routines.

As the World Championship trials drew near, my athletic efforts intensified and I spent many long hours in practice. But my tunnel vision was gone. Life seemed to be on an even keel because outside the doors of the gym were people and experiences that helped me see beyond the parallel bars.

I wish I could say I lost ten pounds and performed brilliantly at the 1974 World Championships. I can't. I qualified as an alternate, attended the training camp, and headed home to complete my senior year at Urbana High School. The seven gymnasts who finished ahead of me went on to compete at the Championships in Sophia, Bulgaria. After all the sacrifices, it was hard to find satisfaction in my unfulfilled goals and poor performances.

But during the flight home, my frustration eased as I reflected on my relationship with the Hills in Eugene and joyfully anticipated seeing family and friends in Illinois. I daydreamed about the many people whom I deeply loved and admired. The high regard I held for them was not because they were flawless, had lots of

money, or got straight *A*s. It was their inner qualities—
honesty, warmth, compassion, and kindness—that en-
deared them to me. Whenever they made mistakes or
fell short of their goals, I didn't think of them as
second-rate citizens. I made allowances for them. With
my own inadequacies in mind, I concluded that I
needed to treat myself with the same dignity.

Like the roots of a tree strengthened as seasons pass,
the roots of my character had stood the test of some
emotional storms. I was a stronger person. The past
year had taught me that the ups and downs of my
athletic career didn't determine my value. Despite my
mistakes, I flew home with a sense of accomplishment.
The year in Eugene had been well spent. Landing in
Illinois, over the sound of the 747 engines I kept hearing
my dad's encouragement: "Nancy, we are most proud
of you because of who you are, not what you do."

PRACTICE MAKES BETTER, NOT PERFECT

Many achievers push for perfection in order to please
others. Accomplishments become their only focus in
life. But achievement simply for the sake of gaining
admiration becomes a bondage. Opinion acts as a jailer
and praise becomes the tag on the key that locks us in
the cell.[3] Why? Because you can never please everybody
all the time.

Some perfectionists, however, are not concerned
about image. They are simply consumed by the will to

win. Being the best is the only way they find satisfaction in life. Embracing the philosophy of legendary football coach Vince Lombardi ("Winning isn't everything, it's the only thing"), some have difficulty enjoying life and themselves when they aren't number one.

Retired Olympic figure skater Rosalynn Sumners, a silver medalist in the 1984 Olympics, candidly recalls her addiction to winning: "When you are an athlete, you live for those highs. You train. You peak and feel wonderful. Then you come crashing down."[4] Rosalynn's "crash" came after the '84 Olympic competition. Embarrassed by her loss to East German Katarina Witt, she wrestled with a deep depression that plagued her long after retiring from amateur competition.

Rosalynn's emotional pain is common among those aspiring for the gold. An important question is, can a natural high be found in places other than the winner's circle?

Yes. Olympic figure skater Janet Lynn experienced many highs beyond the victory stand. Janet was considered America's best hope for a gold medal throughout most of her international amateur skating career. Her dedication to the sport carried her through two Olympic Games and six World Championships.

As a five-time U.S. National Champion, Janet was known for the joy she exhibited even in the tightest competitions and after the toughest losses. How was she able to overcome the need to be perfect and better than everybody else? What enabled her to feel good about herself and her performance even when she didn't win?

The secret was her focus. Her sights weren't locked on beating others. Her aim was to do her best and to convey a message of beauty to her audience. She says:

> Whenever I went on the ice with the feeling, *I want to be better than Karen* [or whoever her fiercest rival was at the time], I didn't communicate the love through skating that I wanted to.
>
> I've been told that my philosophy is really radical in the sports world . . . that Vince Lombardi would turn over in his grave to hear me talk like this. But I can't identify with his slogans, like "Winning . . . is the only thing" and "The only substitute for victory is disgust."

Janet evaluated her efforts by a different criteria:

> There were lots of times when I came off the ice without winning that I wasn't disgusted. It would have been wrong to be disgusted. I had skated well and had given something to the audience, and that, to me, was the point of it all. . . . There's a difference between striving for excellence as a way of interacting with God and with your audience, and gritting your teeth in vengeance to be "better than."

Many people did not understand Janet's motivation. Some were cynical and said, "You can't have that attitude when you're in competition. Come on, Janet, you know you wanted to come home from Sapporo [1972 Olympics] with that gold medal. . . ."

Janet's reply after not receiving the gold was this:

> Yes, I did want a gold medal, but not so I could say I was a better skater than every other girl in the world. I wanted it only because it would have been a symbol of excellence, and it would have given me a lot of chances to tell how Christ has helped me. As a matter of fact, I got those chances anyway, so I didn't really lose anything.

Instead of striving for perfection and fame, Janet's goal was to put forth her best effort. Satisfaction was found in performing her routines and influencing others in a positive fashion.

Janet believed her skating performance was one way to communicate Christ's love to her audience. Her prayer before each routine was for help to "love every minute, every move . . . and to pour love out to the crowd."[5]

Janet maintained a standard of excellence, but the pressures of perfectionism were absent because her focus wasn't on receiving but on giving. Rather than trying to acquire love through success, she acquired success through loving others.

For some it is hard to believe that striving for perfection doesn't guarantee love. Why? Because the results of hard work are often fantastic. After all, "Early to bed,

early to rise, makes a man healthy, wealthy, and wise."
However, the fallacy of this belief is illustrated in certain
life stories where the quest for perfection became a
disappointing burden rather than a blessing.

At the 1986 NCAA Outdoor Track and Field Championships, sports enthusiasts were stunned when one
of the leaders in the women's ten-thousand-meter race
suddenly left the pack of runners, climbed over a fence,
ran two blocks, and jumped off a forty-foot bridge.

Kathy Ormsby was an unlikely candidate for a suicide
attempt. She was successful at almost everything she
did. She graduated number one in her high school class
with a straight A average. Her school named a day of
celebration in her honor after she won the eight-
hundred-, sixteen-hundred-, and thirty-two-hundred-
meter races at the North Carolina State High School
Championships, setting records in all three events. As a
premed student at North Carolina State University,
Kathy's goal was to become a medical missionary. In
her spare time, she was a youth leader and sang in her
church choir. Friends and acquaintances attested to her
sincerity and humility, saying that "she was embarrassed by the adulation" from her successes.

Kathy was well on her way to becoming one of the
nation's best female distance runners. Two months
before the tragedy, she set the women's intercollegiate
ten-thousand-meter record at the Penn Relays. Considered a favorite to win the Collegiate Championships in
Indianapolis, Kathy displayed the makings of a bona

fide all-American heroine. She was well-liked, intelligent, physically strong, and full of faith in God—a seemingly unbeatable combination. But in one split second she experienced the death of her running career.

The fall from the bridge left Kathy paralyzed from the waist down. Those who knew her searched long and hard for answers to the question, "Why?" Kathy's father said she was "an overachiever" who succumbed to "the pressure to succeed."[6] In an interview six months later, Kathy explained that after running about five thousand meters, she felt the NCAA race slipping away from her. The lead group, of which she was a part, began to pull ahead. She desperately tried to keep up the pace, but she felt as if she were hardly moving.

"I saw what was happening as failing God," she told the Charlotte, North Carolina, *Observer.* "I felt like I was failing my coach and my parents and I thought there was something wrong with me."[7]

Unfortunately, the fallacy "Anything less than perfection is intolerable" had somehow lodged itself in the recesses of Kathy's mind. She had learned to find her value in achievements measured by a time clock and adulation rather than in who she was as a person.

Months after the accident, Kathy evaluated and concluded that she didn't have to live in the extremes of black-and-white thinking. "I do think God wants us to do our best. . . . But I don't think He wants us to be obsessed with that or do it in such a way that it doesn't leave time for [us] to enjoy life."[8] She realized that her running didn't have to be an all-or-nothing venture. She was more than a pair of strong legs that beat the pavement faster than others. As a precious individual, uniquely created with strengths and weaknesses, running was simply one expression of her personhood.

Like Kathy, many feel they let God down when falling short of perfection and losing a contest. But God never asks us to win all the time. He simply asks us to do our best. "Whatever you do, do your work heartily, as for the Lord rather than for men" (Colossians 3:23 NAS).

God knows the perils of people pleasing and encourages us to find our motivation for excellence outside this paradigm. He says to work and play with Him in mind, rather than looking for approval from others. Why? Because He knows the liberating power of this mentality. Worrying about what others might think and say costs energy. With God's game plan, that energy can be channeled into healthy endeavors rather than wasted on presumption.

No, God doesn't ask for perfection. He knows that perfection this side of heaven is an impossibility. That is why He gave His life on the cross—not to help those who "had it all together" but to show His love for imperfect humans with frailties. To those who feel defeated, He says, "Come to me, all you who are weary and burdened, and I will give you rest. Take my yoke upon you and learn from me, for I am gentle and humble in heart, and you will find rest for your souls" (Matthew 11:28, 29 NIV).

Perhaps you have been knocked down and are having difficulty getting back up again. Let me remind you that what you do is not nearly as important as who you are. Have you been striving for perfection so you will be accepted by others? Try giving love away instead. Love is like throwing a boomerang: once sent upon its outward course, it will return unerringly to you. Try turning your gaze away from others toward God. The need for human approval vanishes in the security of His unconditional favor. Try to remember that practice makes better, not perfect. As you cease striving for flawlessness and aim for doing your best, the prison doors of perfectionism will fly open and freedom will prevail.

SEVEN

CURTAILING THE CRUSHING POWER OF CRITICISM

"NANCY, I AM concerned about your attitude as a team member. I know you've been successful in the past, but that doesn't give you the right to waltz in here and run the show. Your comments about our program are not appreciated. I won't tolerate any prima donnas on the team."

These words caught me off guard. As a new member of a fledgling gymnastics program, I had enthusiastically offered encouragement to the athletes and suggestions to the staff about improving the equipment in the gym. I thought my contributions were positive, but they obviously weren't well received. I was misunderstood, judged, and then accused of false motives. The sharp attack cut deep.

None of my explanations was going to erase the preconceived image this person had of me. I resented being sentenced without a trial. I wondered if I could continue to support the program with strong feelings of bitterness growing inside me.

Most of us have felt the sting of criticism at one time or another. A high school freshman is laughed at by the self-proclaimed "fashion experts." A young executive's enthusiasm is squelched when her boss delivers a negative evaluation. Parents take a blow from their teenage child when he angrily blurts out, "You're full of it—why don't you pull your heads out of the clouds and join the real world?" An athlete's words are often misunderstood or taken out of context, causing team-mates and fans to turn against him.

There is no escape. Criticism is a fact of life. In the sports world, where athletes are constantly scrutinized by coaches, officials, parents, teammates, and fans, ill-timed words can kill confidence. Left to linger, mem-ories of the criticism simmer inside, heating emotions to the boiling point. The question then becomes not how do we avoid criticism, but how do we learn from it and let go of it?

Some feel that being the object of anger or criticism is intolerable. But many on the cutting edge in their fields have learned to accept correction and consider it objec-tively. Bonnie Blair is one individual who tries to discern whether or not there is any value in the criticism she receives, and embraces reproof for the benefit of her career.

GOOD FOOD FOR THOUGHT

In February 1987, Bonnie broke through the Eastern European domination of speed skating and set a new world record in the five-hundred-meter race. This record and her growing reputation as a top skater in the one-thousand- and fifteen-hundred-meter races makes Bonnie one of America's leading contenders in skating competition.

It is not surprising to hear her say, "Up to this point, breaking the world record is indeed the highlight of my skating career."

Even as a leading competitive speed skater, Bonnie constantly receives criticism. U.S. coach Mike Crowe is quick to find fault while evaluating her performances.

"I'm a technical skater," Bonnie says, "which means every move has to be very precise. I can have the best race of my life and Mike will still make a comment such as, 'You used the right side of your body too much,' or 'You should have worked the turn harder.' "

Some athletes would respond with frustration. "Can't you let me savor my victory? So I made a few mistakes. What's the big deal? Lighten up!"

But Bonnie realizes the value of criticism. "I'm glad Mike points out my inadequacies. If he didn't, I wouldn't improve, and that's my goal in every race: to be technically better."

Bonnie has developed the ability to use each critique as one more opportunity to improve her athletic abilities and to acquire skill in handling what might be an unpleasant evaluation. Bonnie considers criticism one of the keys to her improvement and present stature as a world-class athlete.

Granted, not all criticism is constructive. Some is downright brutal. It is difficult to tolerate malicious jabs and unmerciful accusations that whack away at our self-esteem blow by blow.

Unrelenting criticism almost robbed one athlete-turned-sportscaster of her career ambitions. Fortunately she discovered a valuable insight that prevented her from forfeiting her dreams.

WHEN SHOTS ARE FIRED, KEEP HOLDING ON!

It was midnight on Saturday, August 11, 1984, when a tall, blonde woman left the ABC Sports Broadcast Center in Los Angeles. She had just finished cohosting the final late-night wrap-up of the Summer Olympics. She had just become the first woman to serve as a coanchor of Olympic television coverage, the host of an Olympic event (synchronized swimming), as well as an expert commentator for other swimming competitions. As she walked through the venues, vivid memories of her own Olympic accomplishments made Donna de Varona realize how far she had come.

Donna began her competitive swimming career at age ten. After only three years of training, she became the youngest member of the 1960 Rome Olympic Team as a freestyle sprinter.

She continued to swim for four more years, setting eighteen world records and winning thirty-seven national and numerous international awards. In the 1964 Tokyo Games, Donna dominated the four-hundred-meter Individual Medley, setting an Olympic record. She also garnered an additional gold medal as a part of the world-record-setting Freestyle Relay Team.

Donna recalls:

When I was seventeen, I became the country's first female network sports commentator. Working with "ABC's Wide World of Sports," I covered swimming events. At the time I had high ideals and wanted to make a unique contribution to sports journalism, but acceptance in a male-dominated profession was almost nonexistent.

I had two strikes against me when I began broadcasting. I was inexperienced, and I was a young woman. Criticism flew from every direction. Network executives were reluctant to let me branch out and cover other sports. Producers predicted that I would never be anything other than a swimming analyst.

When I became more visible to the public eye, many people thought they had the right to comment on my career. Though some of the criticism was constructive, much of it was unfairly expressed by people in the business who didn't want me moving in on their territory.

The criticism was especially hard to take when I saw myself improving. It was easy for people to remind me of my weaknesses, but few bothered to point out my improvements. I can count on one hand those who acknowledged my potential. I finally got so tired of fighting the flak that I withdrew from the media scene.

In 1977, Donna refocused her efforts in Washington, D.C. Acting as a special consultant to the U.S. Senate for two years, she helped push through the Amateur Sports Act, which restructured amateur athletics in the United States. She was also a driving force behind the passage of Title IX legislation, designed to offer women equality in sports opportunities.

Though the political challenges were rewarding, Donna missed relating with the athletes through broadcasting. She had a passion for commentating, but also a tremendous fear of the potential criticism.

At first it was hard to acknowledge my desires to broadcast again. I had been bruised, and I was scared. But the longer I was away from the cameras, the more I realized I was letting the approval and disapproval of others determine my life's direction. The opinions of others were blinding my vision. My turning point came when I decided not to give up my rights to pursue my dreams.

I started back slowly, cautiously easing my way back into television. My first assignments were as a reporter with ABC's "Eyewitness News" in New York. When I returned to television, I teamed up with NBC Sports and then rejoined ABC Sports in 1983 to commentate and work during the 1984 Olympics.

Today, Donna continues to cover events for ABC Sports. Her road hasn't been smooth and the criticism hasn't stopped. But as a trailblazer on the front lines of sports journalism, Donna has learned to expect and tolerate the flak: "I don't shrink from it anymore. And more important, I haven't allowed my critics to steal my dreams."

BUILDING BRIDGES WITH EMPATHY

Even if we learn to tolerate criticism, it is often difficult to make amends with those who criticize us. We all have emotional memory banks. Painful criticism is hard to forget. But we can prevent bitterness from accumulating in our accounts by developing empathy with our critics. If we focus on the reason for their accusation rather than on whether it was right or wrong, angry resentments are withdrawn from our memory stores. 1984 Olympic champion Mary Lou

Retton tells how empathy steadied her after she received a powerful scolding from her coach, Bela Karoyli.

During one workout a television crew was present,
taping the training of America's Olympic hopefuls at
Bela's gym in Houston, Texas. Mary Lou was perfecting
her uneven bar routine when her hands slipped and she
knocked her chin on the bar, ripping open her lower lip.
She says:

> I was horrified . . . with this big hole in my mouth
> and blood running down my chin and ABC's right in my
> face getting it all.
>
> Bela comes right over and he looks mad. "Get up, get
> up," he barks. "Go to the bathroom, get out of here." I
> was stunned. That was the first time he'd ever yelled at
> me.
>
> It was awful. . . . My mouth was all swollen; I
> couldn't open it. I went home crying, and that night
> Bela called me up and he yelled at me.
>
> "I cannot believe you. With ABC there, you made
> such a big scandal, like a baby. Don't you ever do this
> again. You got to be a strong athlete, not a scared
> rabbit."
>
> I was packed, ready to go back to Fairmont [West
> Virginia]. I'd been depressed before. . . . This time,
> though, was different. "I'm ready to come home," I told
> my mom. "I don't know if I can take this."
>
> All of a sudden, the doorbell rings and in walks Bela.
> I think, "What now?"
>
> "Oh, honey," he says, giving me a big hug with this

apologetic look on his face. "Oh, I am so sorry." And, of course, everything was fine. Bela was just so scared seeing that big hole in my mouth and all the blood that his first reaction was to get angry.

At that point nothing was going to make me go home.[1]

The verbal beating Mary Lou took from Bela was simply a knee-jerk overreaction to uncontrollable circumstances. But Mary Lou benefited from the experience because it provided an opportunity for her to develop compassion for her coach. Understanding his criticism helped her appreciate Bela more deeply. Had Mary Lou Retton clung to her anger, she would have boarded a flight for West Virginia, cut short her promising gymnastics career, and missed out on one of the most endearing coach-athlete relationships in Olympic history. Fortunately, empathy triumphed and so did she!

THE DISARMING POWER OF HUMILITY

Some people bristle at a hint of criticism. With their self-image on the line, they rise to the occasion, fighting back like cornered animals. But there are those who have been able to "make friends quickly with their opponents" (see Matthew 5:25 NAS). Charlie Jones is one such individual.

Millions watch the various athletic contests Charlie

hosts on NBC. His friendships with athletes around the world make his interviews warm and personal, and his vast knowledge of sports facts enables him to communicate complex events in simple terms.

Appearing weekly on national broadcasts, Charlie is often evaluated by viewers. He concedes:

> There are usually people who find fault in the way I call events. I learned early in my career that there were basically two ways for me to respond to my critics. I could fight back by arguing their negative points and escalate the war between us. Or I could absorb the negative words, call my critics to discuss their evaluations, and prompt a cease-fire. Since retaliating usually makes matters worse, I generally take the other route. Talking with my critics seems to arrest cross fire and gives me a chance to understand their perspective. We generally end our conversations with a greater appreciation for one another. Sometimes seeds of friendship are planted.
>
> My own animosity seems to diminish when I show my accusers their opinions are important to me. It is essential that they know I appreciate both their positive and negative reviews. I realize I'm not perfect, and my professional relationships are better when I acknowledge my weaknesses and potential for error.
>
> Sometimes when I explain my perspective, my critics end up seeing eye-to-eye with me on our original source of conflict. But even if we agree to disagree, I find great

satisfaction knowing I made a deliberate move to bridge the gap between us.

Charlie has learned to skillfully respond to his critics. Rather than retaliating, he chooses to communicate with those who offend him. He approaches his accusers as friends rather than foes. And as the gap between them narrows, animosity disappears beneath bridges of mutual respect and understanding.

I wish Charlie had been around to talk with me when I was criticized for my suggestions about the sports program. I could have used his words of wisdom and saved a tremendous amount of emotional energy that was spent on resentment. I wasted hours asking myself, *What did I do to deserve this? Who do they think they are, talking to me that way?*

Thanks to people like Charlie, I'm less defensive than I used to be because I've learned how to curtail the crushing powers of criticism. I try to determine whether or not the critique has value because sometimes critics offer insight that can help me improve myself.

Over the years, I've also learned that my ability to let go of resentments resulting from criticism depends on how I respond to those who have hurt me. When a critic spouts off, finds fault, or makes an unfair judgment, I now ask myself how I will respond. Will I shrink from the accusations and allow my critics to prevent me from pursuing my goal? Will I retaliate and escalate the war?

Or will I extend myself, try to understand, and make peace quickly with my opponents?

When I'm building bridges, it is essential to know precisely where each side of the river is. Empathy is my instrument for surveying the situation. Humility and respect help me span the gap between the sides. No longer blinded by animosity, I can forge ahead toward excellence.

EIGHT

FILLING
THE VOID
OF LONELINESS

"FRIENDSHIP FIRST, COMPETITION second" isn't often heard in athletic arenas. The desire for faster times, better scores, or longer measurements and the compulsion to win suppress thoughts of supporting and encouraging others. People become a low priority when efforts are focused primarily on statistics and results.

Some athletic stars have said, "It's lonely at the top." But does it have to be? Do pursuits have to come before people? Is it a waste of time and energy to invest in relationships at the expense of performance goals? Are friendships a luxury top athletes can't afford?

The Chinese gymnastics delegation visiting the

United States in 1973 would answer "No!" to each of these questions. When they came to compete in Madison Square Garden, they lived by the "Friendship first, competition second" motto. Their determination to cultivate relationships set the stage for a remarkable international competitive experience.

Socializing with opponents is usually not encouraged until after competition. But the morning before the Chinese-American gymnastics contest, the Chinese delegation invited all of us on the U.S. team to their hotel floor for an authentic oriental breakfast.

We stepped off the elevator that morning into complete chaos. Coaches, officials, athletes, government dignitaries, and Secret Service men crowded the small lobby. Enthusiastically, the Chinese gymnasts approached our team with friendly smiles and linked arms with us. After the interpreters made the introductions, we were whisked away to small decorated tables in the hallway. The genuine hospitality and kindness of the Chinese during our meal almost erased my thoughts and anxieties of the pending competition.

When we met in Madison Square Garden the next day, I was astounded by the support the Chinese team gave each of us. After my first event, as I walked back to the sidelines, the entire Chinese women's team ran out to greet me, offering their hands in congratulations. This had never happened to me in a national or an international meet.

I had been taught to remove myself from competitors'

performances. I wasn't to get caught up in any emotion that might jar my concentration. The Chinese didn't operate that way. They unselfishly extended themselves to others. Even after my falls from the bars and the beam, the Chinese athletes huddled around me, offering hearty pats on my back. My mistakes were overshadowed by their genuine support.

Our intercultural friendships with one another have continued for many years after the competition ended. In 1979, I made the first of three visits to China as a broadcaster for NBC Sports. I was thrilled to see some of the gymnasts I had met in 1973, and they welcomed me to their country with open arms. We had great fun catching up on much that had happened in the interim. During another visit, I spent an afternoon with Chou Chiasheng, his wife, and son. He was the pianist who improvised for me when my taped music didn't play. We exchanged stories about our families and hometowns. I thanked God for the opportunity to step into Mr. Chou's world as he had into mine nine years before.

My Chinese friends made a profound impression on me. They showed me how to look beyond myself and appreciate others. They taught me it was possible to care for people, even opponents, and still strive for peak performances in competition. I didn't win a medal competing against the Chinese in Madison Square Garden, but I came home with a much more treasured prize: an international comradery that transcended competitive differences.

TAKING TIME TO CARE

Another athlete, four-time Olympic runner Madeline Manning Mims, is known for the high priority she places on genuinely caring for others. The beauty of her compassionate heart was seen at the 1968 Olympics in Mexico City.

During a qualifying heat for the eight-hundred-meter final, one of Madeline's toughest competitors, Yugoslavian Vera Nikolic, unexpectedly stopped running after completing three hundred of the eight hundred meters. She walked off the track and climbed the stadium steps in a confused stupor.

Madeline says:

> I found out later that Vera was headed for the bridge outside of the Olympic venue to take her life. Her country had not been very successful in the Games. The Yugoslavian officials were putting great pressure on her to win the gold medal. She simply broke down under the pressure.
>
> The next day I was walking with my teammates to board a bus for the stadium. It was the day of my Olympic final. We passed Vera standing in front of the dormitory, surrounded by two guards and her coach. She was on her way home to Yugoslavia. Even though

she was one of my fiercest competitors, I felt great compassion for her. I told my teammates to go on to the stadium and to relay the message to my coach that I'd catch the next bus. Groping for words to encourage her, I said, "Vera, you are young and your mistakes are behind you. You have many years of running ahead. I care about you, and God loves you, too."

Moments later, Vera was escorted to the airport and Madeline hopped a bus for the stadium. Shortly after, Madeline set a world record while winning the 1968 Olympic gold medal in the eight-hundred-meter event. Madeline says:

I often wondered if I would ever race against Vera again. Our paths didn't cross for a year. But I received my first update on her from the Yugoslavian coach during a meet in Germany. He said that Vera had left the Mexico City Olympics in a catatonic state, unable to communicate with anyone. In Yugoslavia she was hospitalized and received psychiatric treatment for depression. When she finally spoke, her first words were, "Madeline was on her way to compete in the final, and she took the time to talk to me."

"She took the time to talk. . . ." Most athletes going into an Olympic final do everything in their power to avoid people. Socializing breaks concentration. But Madeline went against the norm. Mental preparation for her own race took a backseat when she chose to offer encouragement and hope to her Yugoslavian opponent.

Ironically, the tables were turned on Madeline four years later at the 1972 Munich Olympics. "I was running in my qualifying heat and mistakenly stopped at a marker placed about fifteen feet before the actual finish line. Vera was in the stadium, too, waiting to run in her heat. She saw my confusing finish and ran down to sit with me while the officials were deciding if I qualified for the finals."

When the results were announced, the defending Olympic champion was heartbroken. An unfortunate error blocked Madeline from qualifying for the final and left her devastated.

"Vera hugged me, saying, 'You're young and you can put this mistake behind you.' Then with a twinkle in her eye she said, 'Besides, you have God on your side.' "

Vera's encouragement was invaluable. Madeline recalls, "I needed to hear words of hope. Flashbacks of our talk outside her dormitory in 1968 reminded me that I had used those same words of comfort. Seeing Vera happy and back on her feet again helped to put my loss in perspective. Her presence helped me have faith for brighter tomorrows."

Madeline's and Vera's sensitive affirmations built bridges of love between them. When they each were knocked down, they helped one another up. And in a competitive arena where top awards are considered the ultimate measure of one's value, their friendship reminded them that God, and at least one other person, felt they were special.

Incidentally, Vera, who was the 1972 pre-Olympic favorite, finished in a tie for fifth place.

BROTHER AND SISTER AS BEST FRIENDS

In more recent years, another pair of track-and-field athletes warmed the hearts of Olympic spectators with their spirited support of each other. One of the most endearing friendships of the 1984 Games was shared by an American brother and sister, Al and Jackie Joyner.

They grew up in poverty-stricken East Saint Louis, where opportunities to succeed were limited. Unpleasant memories were etched in Al's and Jackie's minds. Across the street from their modest home was a liquor store and pool hall, which provided townspeople a temporary escape from the pain of despair. The area was also a breeding ground for crime and violence. Jackie witnessed a shooting before she was twelve years old.

Longing to escape their oppressive surroundings, Al and Jackie swore that their lives would be different. In the back room of their family's tiny home, they made a pact: "Someday we are going to make it out of here—we are gonna make things different!"[1]

Their mother, Mary, had the same dream for her four children, and she raised them with solid guidelines and high expectations. Their school work and good relationships were to be top priority. Sports were to be chosen over drugs and alcohol.

From their early childhood, Al and Jackie were gifted with incredible athletic ability. They spent many hours at the community center, participating in a variety of sports. Though Al was the oldest, Jackie was the motivator throughout their high school years.[2] Because of Jackie's persistent prodding, Al reluctantly crawled out of bed for morning track practices. It paid off as he triple-jumped his way to an athletic scholarship at Tennessee State University. He later transferred to Arkansas State.

Two years after Al entered the university, Jackie graduated in the top 10 percent of her high school class. She had an illustrious high school career in basketball, volleyball, and track, setting a state high school record in the long jump her junior year.

In the fall of 1980, a scholarship to UCLA lured Jackie away from East Saint Louis. With the prospect of college educations at reputable schools, and budding athletic careers, the two eldest Joyners were on their way to seeing their dream of "a better life" come true.

But their dream lost its sparkle the following January when Mary, their mother and most dedicated supporter, suddenly contracted a rare form of meningitis. By the time Jackie arrived at the hospital, Mary was in a coma. Several hours later she died.

Life was difficult for Al and Jackie with their mother

gone. Jackie felt an added responsibility to care for her brother and younger sisters.

It wasn't easy for them to be motivated for practices when grief consumed so much of their energy. But as time passed, Jackie embraced her mother's determination in life and became more intense in pursuing her athletic goals. Al dedicated his meets to his mother in memory of the inspiration she was to those who knew her. Whenever it was possible, Al and Jackie attended each other's competitions, offering strong moral support from the sidelines.

Another person who encouraged Jackie during her grief was assistant UCLA track coach Bob Kersee. Having lost his mother when he was Jackie's age, Bob was particularly sensitive to her sorrow. Amazed by Jackie's athletic ability, he didn't want her training to be adversely affected by family pressures.

Coach Kersee encouraged Jackie to train for the heptathlon, a seven-event discipline similar to the men's decathlon. She followed his advice, and less than three years later qualified for the 1983 U.S. World Championships team in that event. Al also qualified for the team in the triple jump, but their performances in the Helsinki competition were disappointing. Al finished eighth in his event and Jackie had to withdraw from competition. Both suffered from pulled hamstring muscles. Trying to comfort Jackie after the Championships, Al told her, "It's just not our time yet."[3]

Following the World Championships, Al moved to

Southern California to train with Jackie under Kersee's tutelage. Brother and sister were a team again, working with a gifted coach. Bound by their dreams and loyalty to each other, they persevered through the final year of pre-Olympic training.

The following summer at the Los Angeles Olympics, Al wasn't considered a favorite for an Olympic medal. Nevertheless, after three of six rounds in the triple jump, he led the group of finalists.

On that same August night, Jackie, the favorite in the heptathlon, was also in the Olympic stadium. She was competing in her final three events, leading Australia's Glynis Nunn by a very slim margin.

As Al was starting his fourth round, Jackie stood across the infield at the starting line of the eight-hundred-meter run, her last event. She was only thirty-one points ahead of Nunn, a small lead by heptathlon standards. According to the elaborate scoring system, Jackie could lose to Nunn by 2.13 seconds or less (which would be about fourteen yards) and still hold on to first place.

When the gun was fired at the beginning of Jackie's race, Al left his triple-jump station and ran to the infield edge of the final turn. The first time Jackie passed she was trailing Nunn, and Al encouraged her to stay close. The second time around she was behind by about twenty yards and he shouted, "Pump your arms, Jackie . . . this is it!"[4]

Her time was only a fraction of a second more than

the time she needed in her final race. She lost the gold medal by five points.

Al must have felt many confusing emotions on that balmy night as he walked back to his triple-jump station. On the one hand, if no one jumped farther than his distance of 56', 7½" in the next three rounds, he would win a gold medal. But, on the other hand, his closest friend and greatest source of encouragement had just lost her last chance of winning the gold.

When the triple jump was completed, the results confirmed that Al's performance had surpassed all others. He was a new Olympic Champion.

After the awards ceremony, Jackie stood arm-in-arm with Al, tears streaming down her face. But she wasn't shedding tears of disappointment. Hugging Al tight, she said, "I'm not crying because I lost. I'm crying because you won. You fooled them all!"[5]

For those of us watching the Olympic events unfold on TV, Jackie's quest seemed as much Al's as her own. To many, the emotional support Al gave Jackie overshadowed his own historic accomplishment of becoming the first American in eighty years to win the triple jump.

Through the years, Al and Jackie have shared many joys and sorrows. In 1986, Al walked Jackie down the aisle when she married her coach, Bob Kersee. Six months later Al rejoiced when Jackie set a new heptathlon world record at the Goodwill Games in Moscow, and again, four weeks later, when she broke that record at the U.S. Olympic Festival.

The following November Jackie was chosen as one of ten finalists for the 1986 Sullivan Award, which honors the amateur athlete of the year. When Joan Benoit, the 1985 winner, announced the name of the 1986 winner, the crowd of over one thousand sports enthusiasts, dignitaries, and Olympic athletes erupted with a standing ovation for Jackie Joyner-Kersee. And no one cheered louder than one particular Olympian seated in the audience who had shared so much with her. Jumping almost as high out of his seat (in a black tuxedo!) as he jumped for his gold medal, Al Joyner applauded Jackie without reserve.

When they were young, Al and Jackie made a friendship pact with each other. As the years passed, they continued to stick together during triumphs and tragedies. They avidly encouraged and challenged one another to do their best. They believed in each other when others did not. They rejoiced for each other under all circumstances. And while supporting one another after their mother's death, their painful injuries, and disappointing losses, "shared sorrow became half-sorrow." Through record-breaking finishes, Olympic award ceremonies, and a wedding celebration, they found that "shared joy becomes double joy." A wise old king once said it another way: "Two are better than one because they have a good return for their labor. For if either of them falls, the one will lift up his companion. But woe to the one who falls when there is not another to lift him up" (Ecclesiastes 4:9, 10 NAS).

AN ETERNAL FRIEND

From the moment I met Jill Johnson and Debbie Halle in gymnastics competition years ago, I knew they were people with a passion for excellence. There was something different about them that made me gravitate in their direction. I was fascinated by their zest for life and openness with others.

The summer after my sophomore year in high school, the three of us taught and roomed together at a gymnastics camp in Wisconsin. As our friendship grew, I soon discovered the predominant reason for their joy: They had a vivacious faith in God unlike anything I'd ever seen before. I hadn't known anyone else my own age who was so enthusiastic about Jesus. They talked about Him as if He were their closest Friend.

I had grown up in a loving family, surrounded by godly people. I had been exposed to Christianity, and as far as I knew was involved in a Christian life-style. But compared with Debbie and Jill, there was a void in my life. They had something I wanted, and that "something" couldn't be found in medals, honors, titles, or other people. It was a peace and joy that could be found only in a relationship with God, the Source of abundant life.

Thanks to these two special people, I made an eternal

friendship that summer with the Lord Jesus Christ. Through Bible study and prayer, I began to discover God's desire to be my Companion—a dependable Friend who provides wise guidance, enduring support, unfailing courage, and championship strength.

Many years have passed since that summer with Debbie and Jill. The triumphs and failures of my athletic career eventually yielded to college pursuits, sports broadcasting, public relations jobs, and the demands of marriage and motherhood. My journey has been a series of ups and downs, sometimes bitter and some- times sweet. But Jesus Christ has walked beside me each step of the way, offering unconditional love when I failed and doubted my abilities to plod forward, comfort when life wasn't fair, confidence when I felt insignificant, courage to extend myself to critics, wis- dom to keep my goals and priorities straight, and eternal friendship when I was lonely.

Do you feel isolated in your pursuits of excellence? Don't neglect people for the sake of pursuits. Invest in relationships. As with most profitable endeavors, friendships don't just happen. They are born and nurtured by people who look beyond themselves and reach out to those around them.

Sensitize yourself to the needs of others. Affirm. Encourage. Look for opportunities to step into someone else's world. For it's when people care for one another, in spite of the good, bad, and ugly, that everyone wins.

Is there a vacuum in your life? Do you sense a need to

find meaning and direction in your endeavors? May I introduce you to a Friend who has an eternal purpose for you? His name is Jesus Christ, and He is eager to become acquainted with you. He offers an invitation to you:

> "I am the way, and the truth, and the life; no one comes to the Father, but through me. . . . Behold, I stand at the door of your heart and I am constantly knocking. If anyone hears me calling him and opens the door, I will come in and fellowship with him and he with me. . . . I will never desert you, nor will I ever forsake you."
>
> John 14:6 NAS; Revelation 3:20 TLB; Hebrews 13:5 NAS

NOTES

CHAPTER 1

BREAKING BARRICADES OF DOUBT

1. Edwin Muller, "Drama in Real Life: She Rode to Triumph Over Polio," *Reader's Digest*, vol. 67, no. 400, August 1955, pp. 59–62.

CHAPTER TWO

SOFTENING THE BLOWS OF INJUSTICE

1. "Local Girls on U.S. Team," *Champaign-Urbana Courier*, May 30, 1971, sec. III, p. 14.
2. Scott Craven, "Rhythmic Gymnast Sue Soffe," *Olympian*, vol. 8, no. 8, March 1982, pp. 16, 17.
3. Michele Kort, "Best Bets From the U.S.," *Women's Sports*, vol. 5, no. 10, October 1983, p. 36.
4. "Stars and Strides," *Olympian*, vol. 1, no. 1, July/August 1974, p. 6.
5. Richard Hoffer, "Tai and Randy Feeling Richer Without

the Gold," *Los Angeles Times*, February 14, 1984, sec. III, pp. 1, 6.

CHAPTER FOUR

ESCAPING THE EVILS OF ENVY

1. The fourth-place finish was the highest by an American women's gymnastics team in the sport as it is known today. The U.S. women earned a medal in the 1948 Olympics for their performance in the group exercise, which is no longer included in Women's Artistic Gymnastics.
2. Gordy Holt, "Joan Rice Retains Title in Gymnastics," *Seattle-Post Intelligencer*, May 5, 1973, sec. B, p. 2.

CHAPTER FIVE

CONQUERING THE VICTIM MENTALITY

1. Amy Bernhard, "Sledding Toward Sarajevo," *California Living* magazine in the *San Francisco Sunday Examiner and Chronicle*, December 4, 1983, pp. 16–22.
2. Tom FitzGerald, "The Bay Area Roots of Top U.S. Lugers," *San Francisco Chronicle*, February 7, 1984, sec. A, p. 44.
3. Frank Litsky, "Bonny Warner's $8 Investment Matures," *New York Times*, February 5, 1984, sec. 5, p. 4.
4. William Johnson, "And Smile, Smile, Smile," *Sports Illustrated*, June 4, 1973, vol. 38, no. 22, p. 78.
5. "ABC's Wide World of Sports," May 1973, Chinese-American Gymnastics Competition, Gordon Maddox, color analyst.

CHAPTER SIX

PUTTING ASIDE PERFECTIONISM

1. *Webster's New Collegiate Dictionary* (Springfield, Massachusetts: G. & C. Merriam Company, 1973), p. 51.
2. Willard Hansen, "Nancy Thies Aims for 1976 Olympics," *Champaign-Urbana News Gazette,* November 12, 1972, sec. 4, p. 37.
3. Karen Burton Maines, *With My Whole Heart* (Portland, Oregon: Multnomah Press, 1987), p. 123.
4. Judy Mills, "Cracking Up," *Women's Sports and Fitness,* vol. 8, no. 10, October 1986, p. 46.
5. Janet Lynn With Dean Merrill, *Peace and Love, Janet Lynn* (Carol Stream, Illinois: Creation House, 1973), pp. 66, 67. Reprinted with permission from Janet Lynn Salomon.
6. Tom Minehart, "Ormsby 'Dedicated Overachiever' Done in by Will to Succeed," *Portland Oregonian,* June 15, 1986, sec. E, p. 14.
7. "Ormsby Explains Suicide Attempt," *Los Angeles Times,* December 22, 1986, sec. III, p. 19.
8. "Answers Not Easy as Ormsby Reflects," *New York Times,* December 22, 1986, sec. C, p. 9.

CHAPTER SEVEN

CURTAILING THE CRUSHING POWER OF CRITICISM

1. Mary Lou Retton and Bela Karolyi With John Powers, *Mary Lou: Creating an Olympic Champion* (New York: McGraw-Hill Book Company, 1986), pp. 83, 84.

CHAPTER EIGHT

FILLING THE VOID OF LONELINESS

1. Kenny Moore, "Ties That Bind," *Sports Illustrated*, April 27, 1987, vol. 66, no. 17, p. 78.
2. Patricia Freeman, "Is She the Greatest of Them All?" *Women's Sports and Fitness*, vol. 9, no. 1, January 1987, p. 57.
3. Moore, p. 84.
4. Ibid.
5. Ibid.